LEGAL ISSUES JOURNAI
Volume 9, Issue 1
January 2022

AF688036

Legal Issues Journal (LIJ) is a not-for-profit peer reviewed inter-disciplinary journal publishing original research in law, as well as inter-disciplinary research at the intersection of law and other disciplines, including genetics, biosciences, philosophy, linguistics, neuroscience, medicine and ethics. The core aim of the LIJ is to disseminate knowledge that contributes towards achieving justice – free from commercial considerations. The Journal publishes original papers, case comments, short reports, debates and book reviews. The Journal also provides interpretation articles on changes in the legal world and coming trends affecting law, lawyers, and society.

ISBN: 979-8-215-03341-8

ISSN 2516-1210
ISSN 2515-9887

LEGAL ISSUES JOURNAL 9(1)

UKLSA

The UK Law & Society Association

SULIS ACADEMIC PRESS

An Imprint of Sulis International
Los Angeles | Dallas | London
www.sulisinternational.com

Legal Issues Journal 9(1)

The United Kingdom Law and Society Association (UKLSA)

www.uklsa.co.uk

Table of Contents

Legal Issues Journal 9(1) 2022: 1–13.

The Liability Limits of Self-Driving Cars

Liliya Ivanova[1], Nikita Kalashnikov[2]

ABSTRACT. This article presents and discusses recent developments of using autonomous vehicles and analyses their effectiveness in terms of the theory of criminal responsibility for harm caused. The authors consider the liability of the autopilot according to several theoretical approaches. The main approaches assume liability for injury caused during the operation of the elevator, responsibility for damage caused by autopilots of large transport, and the charge of the human driver. There are some types of criminal liability concerning harm caused by autonomous vehicles. One way relates to using partially autonomous cars where a human driver is always responsible for driving. In the case of road incidents, only the human driver might be found guilty. In the case of full automation, when a human driver does not control the vehicle, be it autopilot as a self-learning program or not, only the developer or the technicians should be responsible in case of harm. Another case is related to the behaviour of the owner of the autonomous vehicle. The authors conclude that legal regulation is necessary. A separate corpus delicti as a new article is needed in the criminal legislation to provide criminal liability for death or other grave consequences caused by unmanned vehicles.

Keywords: Self-driving car; Autopilot; Criminal liability; Autonomous vehicle

---

[1]University of Tyumen. Corresponding author: Liliya Ivanova, ivanova_liliya@mail.ru.
[2]University of Tyumen.

Self-driving cars, or unmanned vehicles, are rapidly making their way into our everyday life. The following circumstances explain this trend. Firstly, unmanned vehicles may be convenient for drivers who may wish to multitask whilst driving. Drivers may read and write messages, prepare for a work meeting, or relax. Multitasking during a commute may increase worker productivity[3]. Secondly, according to some research[4], manned vehicles are much safer on the road because an autopilot does not get tired, intoxicated, or distracted as does the human driver[5]. Based on this, technological developments of this kind are promising for the future of humankind.

However, with the rapid development of science and technology, the public safety of autonomous vehicles must be considered. There are issues in terms of the legal regulation of autonomous vehicles and the definition of responsible limits on road incidents[6]. What is the legal status of autonomous vehicles? Who is liable in the case of road incidents with self-driving cars: the autopilot, the driver, the manufacturer, the programmer, or someone else?

Before addressing these issues, it is necessary to understand the terminology. Autonomous and unmanned vehicles are frequently confused with cars that are only equipped with technologies that help the driver. From a legal perspective, such confusion is unacceptable given the growing number of autonomous cars and the arising legal repercussions related to safety and ethics[7]. While self-driving cars are not in operation, instances of vehicles

---

[3]LeValley, D. (2013). Autonomous Vehicle Liability – Application of Common Carrier Liability. *Seattle University Law Review*, 36. P. 5.

[4]Yoganandhan, A., Subhashs, S.D., Hebinson, J. & Mohanavel, V. (2020). Fundamentals and development of self-driving cars. *Materials today: proceedings.* DOI: 10.1016/j.matpr.2020.04.736.

[5]Gurney, J.K. (2013). Sue My Car Not Me: Products Liability and Accidents Involving Autonomous Vehicles. University of Illinois Journal of Law, Technology & Policy, 2. P. 251.

[6]Hevelke, A., Nida-Rümelin, J. (2015). Responsibility for Crashes of Autonomous Vehicles: An Ethical Analysis. *Science and Engineering Ethics,* 21, Pp. 619–630. DOI: 10.1007/s11948-014-9565-5.

[7]Statista Logo. Placek, M. (2021). Projected number of autonomous cars globally 2019-2024. www.statista.com/statistics/1230664/projected-number-autonomous-cars-worldwide/ (accessed 27th January 2022).

riding on lanes autonomously and slowing down at the sight of obstacles, as well as parking themselves, have been reported[8]. The newest models, such as Audi Q7, Q8, BMW X7, Tesla Model 3, X, Y, Volkswagen Atlas, Volvo XC90, and others, already have autonomous technologies. These cars are often called "unmanned vehicles".

Many drivers succumb to marketing strategies and appealing narratives about vehicles that are "autonomous" and can drive on public roads on their own. Such drivers treat assistance technologies irresponsibly and may create dangerous emergencies[9]. Autopilot is only an assist feature. For example, Tesla noticed that the autopilot system is not intended to replace the driver but for fully attentive driving, where the driver's hands are on the wheel and is prepared to take over at any time[10].

Media analysis shows that the large-scale integration of partially autonomous cars into public life has begun. The main manufacturers (in addition to industry leader Tesla), such as BMW[11], General Motors[12], Volvo[13], and KAMAZ[14] have already launched their

---

[8]Cars.com. Meier, A. (2021). Which Cars Have Self-Driving Features for 2021? www.cars.com/articles/which-cars-have-self-driving-features-for-2021-433821/ (accessed 27th January 2022).

[9]Hertfordshire Constabulary (2018). News and appeals. Man disqualified from driving after turning on autopilot and leaving driver's seat. www.herts.police.uk/news-and-appeals/man-disqualified-from-driving-after-turning-on-autopilot-and-leaving-drivers-seat (accessed 27th January 2022).

[10]Tesla, Inc. (2020). Tesla Press Information. www.tesla.com/en_EU/presskit/autopilot?redirect=no (accessed 18th July 2020).

[11]BMW. The path to autonomous driving. (2020). www.bmw.com/en/automotive-life/autonomous-driving.html (accessed 18th July 2020).

[12]CNBC. Wayland, M., Kolodny, L. (2020). Debut of GM's Cruise Origin shows the future of ride-sharing, autonomous vehicles is a box. www.cnbc.com/2020/01/23/debut-of-gms-cruise-origin-shows-the-future-of-ride-hailing-autonomous-vehicles-is-a-box.html (accessed 18th July 2020).

[13]Holmes, J. (2011). Volvo Says Autonomous Car Convoys Could Be Reality By 2020. *Motortrend.* www.motortrend.com/news/volvo-autonomous-car-convoys-could-be-reality-2020-80731/ (accessed 18th July 2020).

[14]Voronina, Yu. (2015). Brains on Wheels. *Russian Newspaper.* www.rg.ru/2015/02/10/mozgi.html (accessed 18th July 2020).

full-scale serial production. In addition, companies, including but not limited to Google[15], Yandex[16], Uber[17], and Waymo[18], have been working continuously on autopilots[19].

The level of automatization may differ, and ranges from partial automation and permanent supervising by the driver to full automation and no supervising activity by the driver[20]. To avoid misunderstandings of the terminology, the National Highway Traffic Safety Administration and Society of Automotive Engineers have adopted six driving levels[21]. Level 0 implies a complete lack of automation, whereas level 5 means full automation without a driver. Now, only second-level cars, which assume partial automation, the requirement of constant control, and driver intervention, can be found on public roads. The car driver should always keep his hands on the steering wheel.

Despite the lack of fully autonomous cars on public roads (above level 3 according to the named classification), the present research will include cars with partial (but in the situation when autopilot drives a car) and full automation. The terms "unmanned

---

[15]Google official blog. What we're driving at. (2010). www.googleblog.blogspot.com/2010/10/what-were-driving-at.html (accessed 18th July 2020).

[16]TASS, news-agency. Yandex began testing unmanned vehicles on the Moscow roads. (2019). www.tass.ru/ekonomika/6570313 (accessed 18th July 2020).

[17]Carson, B. (2017). Uber's self-Driving cars hit 2 million miles as program regains momentum. *Forbes Media LLC.* www.forbes.com/sites/bizcarson/2017/12/22/ubers-self-driving-cars-2-million-miles/#17282deea4fe (accessed 18th July 2020).

[18]Pressman, A. (2020). Waymo reaches 20 million miles of autonomous driving. *Fortune.* www.fortune.com/2020/01/07/googles-waymo-reaches-20-million-miles-of-autonomous-driving/ (accessed 18th July 2020).

[19]Gurney, J.K. (2013). Sue My Car Not Me: Products Liability and Accidents Involving Autonomous Vehicles. University of Illinois Journal of Law, Technology & Policy, 2. Pp. 252-253.

[20]Watzenig, D. & Horn, M. (2017). *Automated Driving.* Springer International Publishing. Switzerland. P. 4 DOI 10.1007/978-3-319-31895-0.

[21]Davies, A. (2016). Everyone Wants a Level 5 Self-Driving Car – Here's What That Means. www.wired.com/2016/08/self-driving-car-levels-sae-nhtsa/ (accessed 8th June 2020).

vehicle", "autonomous car", and "self-driving car" are used synonymously.

Motor vehicles with self-driving mode promise sustainable, safe, and efficient mobility for all[22]. The main advantages of using autonomous vehicles are minimizing accidents on roads, the possibility of using the car in any state of health (for example, in case of disability), as well as the possibility of goods transportation in dangerous areas. However, despite these advantages and many years of experience in testing autonomous vehicles, accidents occur. Sometimes accidents end in death and the question of criminal liability rises. The problem of the legal nature of unmanned cars can negate all its advantages.

Before considering liability limits, it is interesting to describe some self-driving car incidents. For example, on May 7, 2016, in the United States, a Tesla Model S, with the autopilot system turned on, fell into a fatal accident. Neither Autopilot nor the driver noticed the white side of the tractor-trailer against a brightly lit sky, so the brake was not applied. Tesla driver died[23]. The commission stated that the driver violated the Tesla user agreement, however, it did not admit to any faults of the vehicle.

Pedestrian death by a self-driving car was first reported in 2018. Elaine Herzberg was struck by an Uber-operated autonomous car while walking her bike across the street[24]. The investigation showed that the car detected the woman as an obstacle and 1.3 seconds before the accident determined the need to use the brakes but did not take any action[25]. Further inspections showed

---

[22]Hartwig, M. *Self-driving and cooperative cars.* BMW. Germany. P. 39. www.bmw.com/content/dam/bmw/marketBMWCOM/bmw_com/categories/Innovation/ebook-self-driving-cars/pdf/e-book-self-driving-cars_en.pdf.asset.1578326516692.pdf (accessed 18th July 2020).

[23]Tesla, Inc. A Tragic Loss. (2016). www.tesla.com/blog/tragic-loss (accessed 8th May 2020).

[24]Griggs, T. & Wakabayashi, D. (2018). How a Self-Driving Uber Killed a Pedestrian in Arizona. *The New York Times.* www.nytimes.com/interactive/2018/03/20/us/self-driving-uber-pedestrian-killed.html (accessed 8th May 2020).

[25]Efrati, A. (2018). Uber Finds Deadly Accident Likely Caused By Software Set to Ignore Objects On Road. *The Information.* www.theinformation.com/articles/uber-finds-deadly-accident-likely-caused-by-software-set-to-ignore-objects-on-road?shared=6c88fd (accessed 8th May 2020).

that Uber engineers deliberately turned off the automatic use of emergency brakes to avoid control conflicts between human drivers and the autopilot. But the video of a dashboard camera showed that the driver was distracted and was looking down from the road[26]. Consequently, the National Transportation Safety Board found the driver of the vehicle guilty, as he did not monitor the road and did not keep his hand on the steering wheel[27]. Elaine Herzberg' death was the result of a set of more distant choices about technology and how it should be developed[28].

In Russia, the first accident caused by the autopilot of the Tesla electric car occurred in 2019. A Tesla Model 3 crashed into a truck and caught fire. The driver and the car passengers received minor injuries. It was later determined that several factors caused the accident. The vehicle was driving at a speed of approximately 100 km/h and could not identify the truck due to the incorrect location on the roadway; meanwhile, the driver distracted on the children[29].

These fatal crashes involving partially autonomous cars strongly suggest that not only autopilot technology is imperfect, but also that there are gaps in the legislative regulations of the liability of unmanned cars for damage caused.

Scientists and self-driving automobile manufacturers consider the liability of the autopilot according to several theoretical approaches. These approaches consider the applicability of actual mechanisms for compensation for harm caused in various life areas to determine liability for damage caused by an unmanned ve-

---

[26]Griggs, T. & Wakabayashi, D. (2018). How a Self-Driving Uber Killed a Pedestrian in Arizona. *The New York Times*. www.nytimes.com/interactive/2018/03/20/us/self-driving-uber-pedestrian-killed.html (accessed 8th May 2020).

[27]National Transportation Safety Board. NTSB News Release (2019). www.ntsb.gov/news/press-releases/Pages/NR20191119c.aspx (accessed 8th May 2020).

[28]Stilgoe, J. (2020). *Who's Driving Innovation?* Palgrave Macmillan. Switzerland. P. 2. DOI 10.1007/978-3-030-32320-2.

[29]TJ. Tesla caught fire and exploded after a collision on the Moscow Ring Road (2019). www.tjournal.ru/news/110821-tesla-zagorelas-i-vzorvalas-posle-stolknoveniya-na-mkade (accessed 8th May 2020).

hicle [30]. The main theories assume liability for injury caused during the operation of the elevator, responsibility for damage caused by autopilots of large transport, the charge of the human driver and others.

The first approach is since liability for injury caused during the elevator operation lies not with the elevator passenger but with the operator or manufacturer. Insurance companies created special elevator liability insurance[31].Elon Musk draws an analogy between accidents involving self-driving vehicles and the emergency mechanism of elevators which forces them to stop moving. However, Musk considers that the lift manufacturer has no liability for all elevators around the world[32]. But being inside an elevator in emergency mode, individuals may be able to win a case against the lift installer or the maintenance. However, it is the driver's responsibility to retain control over the vehicle and to navigate it, ensuring its safe operation on the road. In other words, the control over the autonomous vehicle lies with the vehicle's driver. Tesla has repeatedly pointed out the inadmissibility of negligent use of autonomous technologies. So, the approach based on the liability for injury caused during the elevator operation may not be suitable for unmanned cars since it does not take into account the responsibility of the individual.

Another proposition states that the fatality of accidents should be guided by standards regulating liability for damage caused by autopilots of large transport (ships, aircraft, metro, trains)[33]. This approach considers car systems as a person control. In this case, the responsibility lies with the manufacturer, unless the driver is found guilty of negligence. Many of the crashes appear to involve driver behavior factors, including driving at high speed, mode con-

---

[30]Gurney, J.K. (2013). Sue My Car Not Me: Products Liability and Accidents Involving Autonomous Vehicles. *University of Illinois Journal of Law, Technology & Policy*, 2.

[31]LeValley, D. (2013). Autonomous Vehicle Liability – Application of Common Carrier Liability. Seattle University Law Review, 36. P. 11.

[32]Muoio, D. (2016) Elon Musk: Tesla not liable for driverless car crashes unless it's design related. Business Insider. www.businessinsider.com/elon-musk-tesla-liable-driverless-car-crashes-2016-10 (accessed 27th January 2022).

[33]LeValley, D. (2013). Autonomous Vehicle Liability – Application of Common Carrier Liability. *Seattle University Law Review*, 36.

fusion, and distraction[34]. If the foresight of inappropriate autopilot use is proven (for example, when selling an unmanned vehicle to a driver without experience) the manufacturer of the respective vehicle might be liable too[35]. This approach might not apply to self-driving cars right now because there are second-level cars on public roads, which assume partial automation. And it is mandatory to keep hands on the steering wheel while using an automatic system. So, if the hands of the car driver are not on the steering wheel, the driver can be guilty in case of any road incident..

The third theory approves the application of legislation on sources of increased danger to unmanned vehicles. For example, in Russian Criminal Law all vehicles are always considered dangerous and drivers must take extra care while driving.

Some authors propose to consider autopilot as artificial intelligence capable of learning and adapting over time, indicating in both cases that they are just assistance and semi-intelligent tools in the hands of a person[36]. These tools can create rights and obligations for the owner (by analogy with slaves in ancient Rome). But this approach seems unethical due to the number of parties involved: a car manufacturer or a software designer or a proprietor.

It is important to consider how criminal liability limits for damage caused by unmanned vehicles can be determined. One way relates to using partially autonomous vehicles where a human driver is always responsible for driving. In the case of road incidents, only the human driver might be found guilty. In such instance, an article of the Criminal Code provides liability for the violation of

[34]See e.g. National Highway Traffic Safety Administration. Traffic Safety Facts Research Note (2020). https://crashstats.nhtsa.dot.gov/Api/Public/ViewPublication/813060 (accessed 27th January 2022).

[35]National Highway Traffic Safety Administration. ODI Resume. Investigation PE 16-007 (2016). https://static.nhtsa.gov/odi/inv/2016/INCLA-PE16007-7876.PDF (accessed 8th May 2020).

[36]Churilov, A (2018). The Legal Basis of Liability for the Damage Caused During the Operation of an Autonomous Vehicle. *Legal Concept*, 4. DOI: doi.org/10.15688/lc.jvolsu.2018.4.4.

traffic rules can be adopted, similar to Art. 264 of the Criminal Code of the Russian Federation[37].

A different way relates to using fully autonomous vehicles, including autopilots as artificial intelligence. In this case, the autopilot decides not based on an algorithm provided by the developer but based on its experience. However, any invention, including artificial intelligence, is primarily the result of human intellectual activity, and a person should be liable for possible consequences. Therefore, the developers or technicians of autopilot programs during maintenance should be responsible for future car accidents.

Meanwhile, the safety of autonomous car operations depends on a number of human agencies: developers, technicians, controllers, programmers, vehicle owners, passengers, who are exercising direct control over the safety of its operation[38].

But there may also be a wide variability among potential accidents. For example, if specific algorithm generates situation-specific responses, then the liability may be with the developer.

This is not the case with self-learning neural networks or artificial intelligence. In such instances, the autopilot does not act based on an algorithm provided by the developer but a self-generated one, based on its observations, experience, and data gathered by the vehicle systems. Furthermore, the likelihood of road traffic injuries must be considered. In a potential incident, the autopilot should be assumed responsibility because the developer designed one decision, but the neural network made a completely different decision. It is possible if the programmer builds an open-ended system that can learn from its experience. So, conse-

---

[37]Article 264 of the Criminal Code of the Russian Federation No 63-FL Year 1996 concerning Violation of the Rules for Traffic Safety and Operation of Transport Vehicles provides in part 1 of the Article that "Violation of the rules for traffic safety and operation of transport vehicles by a person driving a car or a train, or any other mechanical transport vehicle, which has involved by negligence the infliction of grave injury to human health shall be punishable by deprivation of liberty for a term of up to two years". A more severe punishment is in case of death, driver intoxication and leaving a place of road incident.

[38]Korobeev, A., Chuchaev, A. (2019). Unmanned vehicles: new challenges to public security. *Lex Russica,* 2. P. 2. DOI: 10.17803/1729-5920.2019.147.2.009-028.

quences of its potential future actions might not be entirely predictable[39].

The following solution is proposed: since a neural network is trained thanks to a vast experience and the analysis of relevant situations, legal regulation is necessary. Law should regulate the self-driving car industry at all stages of production, fixing rules and obligations for everyone. In this case, if violations are detected during the training of the neural network, criminal liability of the autonomous technology developer must be considered. If the developer executes all rules and procedures, then the responsibility lies with the self-learning artificial intelligence.

But it is difficult to assign guilt to a neural network. Any innovation is primarily the result of the intellectual activity of a person or a group of people[40]. Therefore, even in the case of full automation, when the vehicle is not controlled by a human driver, be it autopilot as a self-learning program or not, only the developer or the technicians should be responsible in case of harm. It is assumed that in the future it will be possible to build robots that merit legal personhood and thus can be held liable[41].

Another case is related to the behavior of the owner of the autonomous vehicle. If the owner fails to perform the required annual maintenance in time, as a result of which the autopilot program malfunctions and autopilot harms a pedestrian, then the developer's responsibility is not assumed. The absence of a human driver in a fully autonomous car makes it impossible to prosecute a driver since an individual did not violate the traffic rules. However, failure to complete the maintenance in time could affect the malfunction of the program. There is no specific corpus delicti applic-

---

[39]Alaieri, F., Vellino, A. (2016) Ethical Decision Making in Robots: Autonomy, Trust and Responsibility. In: Agah A., Cabibihan JJ., Howard A., Salichs M., He H. (eds) Social Robotics. ICSR 2016. Lecture Notes in Computer Science, vol. 9979. Springer, Cham. DOI: 10.1007/978-3-319-47437-3_16.

[40]Nekrasov, V.N. (2019). Criminal liability of robots: current problems and directions for further development. *State and Law*, 5. P. 137. DOI: 10.31857/S013207690004886-6.

[41]Lin, P., Abney, K. & Jenkins, R. (2017). *Robot Ethics 2.0: From Autonomous Cars to Artificial Intelligence.* Oxford University Press. New York, NY. P. 67-79. DOI: 10.1093/oso/9780190652951.001.0001.

able to such situations in Russian criminal law. It seems that a separate corpus delicti as a new article is needed in the criminal legislation to provide criminal liability for death or other grave consequences caused by unmanned vehicles.

Law enforcement officials and scientists involved in this case pay attention not only to the problems related to responsibility but also to the issues of using such cars as a means or weapon to commit a crime (murder, property damage, kidnapping, violation of privacy, hijacking and others)[42]. A person may use the remote control on autopilot without being in the car. For instance, in the case of murder, it is possible to shift responsibility to the autopilot, indicating system failure. For hijacking unmanned vehicles, it is enough to get control remotely. Also, cameras installed in unmanned vehicles can potentially be spy tools and violate privacy with the resulting blackmail. These cases are unrealistic but may pose a potential threat in hacking autonomous systems of unmanned vehicles.

In most countries, autonomous cars are banned for use on public roads, but this decision slows down the development of science and technology. Therefore, Russia, like other countries, seeks to create a regulatory framework for self-driving vehicles. Innovations require legislative regulation of their use and liability in case of harm. Firstly, it is necessary to provide a clear definition what an unmanned vehicle is: a partially self-driving vehicle, and autopilot. Secondly, it is important to consolidate the legal status of such means as sources of increased danger.

Arguably, it is possible to evaluate the autopilot actions according to the principle of unconditional personal responsibility of the driver, who is in the car despite the fact that the autopilot may be driving the vehicle. It is more difficult to resolve the issue of liability for fully autonomous cars, assuming their widespread use is without real drivers. In this case, the developer or the proprietor may be responsible for autopilot errors in the future. The question of dealing with guilt in this case seems to require further research.

---

[42]Kufleva, V.N., Sobolev, D.V. & Firsov, V.N. (2019). Problematic aspects of qualifying crimes using an unmanned vehicle. *Man: crime and punishment*, 3. P. 341. DOI: 10.33463/1999-9917.2019.27(1-4).3.335-342.

References

Alaieri, F., Vellino, A. (2016) Ethical Decision Making in Robots: Autonomy, Trust and Responsibility. In: Agah A., Cabibihan JJ., Howard A., Salichs M., He H. (eds) Social Robotics. ICSR 2016. Lecture Notes in Computer Science, vol. 9979. Springer, Cham. DOI: 10.1007/978-3-319-47437-3_16.

BMW. The path to autonomous driving. (2020). www.bmw.com/en/automotive-life/autonomous-driving.html (accessed 18th July 2020).

Carson, B. (2017). Uber's self-Driving cars hit 2 million miles as program regains momentum. Forbes Media LLC. www.forbes.-com/sites/bizcarson/2017/12/22/ubers-self-driving-cars-2-million-miles/#17282deea4fe (accessed 18th July 2020).

Cars.com. Meier, A. (2021). Which Cars Have Self-Driving Features for 2021? www.cars.com/articles/which-cars-have-self-driving-features-for-2021-433821/ (accessed 27th January 2022).

CNBC. Wayland, M., Kolodny, L. (2020). Debut of GM's Cruise Origin shows the future of ride-sharing, autonomous vehicles is a box. www.cnbc.com/2020/01/23/debut-of-gms-cruise-origin-shows-the-future-of-ride-hailing-autonomous-vehicles-is-a-box.html (accessed 18th July 2020).

Churilov, A (2018). The Legal Basis of Liability for the Damage Caused During the Operation of an Autonomous Vehicle. Legal Concept, 4. Pp. 30 – 34. DOI: https://doi.org/10.15688/lc.jvolsu.2018.4.4.

Davies, A. (2016). Everyone Wants a Level 5 Self-Driving Car – Here's What That Means. www.wired.com/2016/08/self-driving-car-levels-sae-nhtsa/ (accessed 8th June 2020).

Efrati, A. (2018). Uber Finds Deadly Accident Likely Caused By Software Set to Ignore Objects On Road. The Information. www.theinformation.com/articles/uber-finds-deadly-accident-likely-caused-by-software-set-to-ignore-objects-on-road?shared=6c88fd (accessed 8th May 2020).

Google official blog. What we're driving at. (2010). www.googleblog.blogspot.com/2010/10/what-were-driving-at.html (accessed 18th July 2020).

Griggs, T. & Wakabayashi, D. (2018). How a Self-Driving Uber Killed a Pedestrian in Arizona. The New York Times. www.nytimes.com/interactive/2018/03/20/us/self-driving-uber-pedestrian-killed.html?action=click&contentCollection=Technology&module=RelatedCoverage&region=Marginalia&pgtype=article (accessed 8th May 2020).

Gurney, J.K. (2013). Sue My Car Not Me: Products Liability and Accidents Involving Autonomous Vehicles. University of Illinois Journal of Law, Technology & Policy, 2. Pp. 247 – 277.

Hartwig, M. Self-driving and cooperative cars. BMW. Germany. 57 p. www.bmw.com/content/dam/bmw/marketBMWCOM/bmw_com/categories/Innovation/ebook-self-driving-cars/pdf/e-book-self-driving-cars_en.pdf.asset.1578326516692.pdf (accessed 18th July 2020).

Hertfordshire Constabulary (2018). News and appeals. Man disqualified from driving after turning on autopilot and leaving driver's seat. www.herts.police.uk/news-and-appeals/man-disqualified-from-driving-after-turning-on-autopilot-and-leaving-drivers-seat (accessed 27th January 2022).

Hevelke, A., Nida-Rümelin, J. (2015). Responsibility for Crashes of Autonomous Vehicles: An Ethical Analysis. Science and Engineering Ethics, 21, Pp. 619–630. DOI: 10.1007/s11948-014-9565-5.

Holmes, J. (2011). Volvo Says Autonomous Car Convoys Could Be Reality By 2020. Motortrend. www.motortrend.com/news/volvo-autonomous-car-convoys-could-be-reality-2020-80731/ (accessed 18th July 2020).

Korobeev, A., Chuchaev, A. (2019). Unmanned vehicles: new challenges to public security. Lex Russica, 2. Pp. 9 – 28. DOI: 10.17803/1729-5920.2019.147.2.009-028.

Kufleva, V.N., Sobolev, D.V. & Firsov, V.N. (2019). Problematic aspects of qualifying crimes using an unmanned vehicle. Man: crime and punishment, 3. Pp. 335 – 342. DOI: 10.33463/1999-9917.2019.27(1-4).3.335-342.

LeValley, D. (2013). Autonomous Vehicle Liability – Application of Common Carrier Liability. Seattle University Law Review, 36. Pp. 5 – 26.

Lin, P., Abney, K. & Jenkins, R. (2017). Robot Ethics 2.0: From Autonomous Cars to Artificial Intelligence. Oxford University Press. New York, NY. 397 p. DOI: 10.1093/oso/9780190652951.001.0001.

Muoio, D. (2016) Elon Musk: Tesla not liable for driverless car crashes unless it's design related. Business Insider. www.businessinsider.com/elon-musk-tesla-liable-driverless-car-crashes-2016-10 (accessed 27th January 2022).

National Highway TrafficSafety Administration. ODI Resume. Investigation PE 16-007 (2016). www.static.nhtsa.gov/odi/inv/2016/INCLA-PE16007-7876.PDF (accessed 8th May 2020).

National Highway Traffic Safety Administration. Traffic Safety Facts Research Note (2020). www.crashstats.nhtsa.dot.gov/Api/Public/ViewPublication/813060 (accessed 27th January 2022).

National Transportation Safety Board. NTSB News Release (2019). www.ntsb.gov/news/press-releases/Pages/NR20191119c.aspx (accessed 8th May 2020).

Nekrasov, V.N. (2019). Criminal liability of robots: current problems and directions for further development. State and Law, 5. P. 134 – 140. DOI: 10.31857/S013207690004886-6.

Pressman, A. (2020). Waymo reaches 20 million miles of autonomous driving. Fortune. www.fortune.com/2020/01/07/googles-waymo-reaches-20-million-miles-of-autonomous-driving/ (accessed 18th July 2020).

Voronina, Yu. (2015). Brains on Wheels. Russian Newspaper. www.rg.ru/2015/02/10/mozgi.html (accessed 18th July 2020).

Statista Logo. Placek, M. (2021). Projected number of autonomous cars globally 2019-2024. www.statista.com/statistics/1230664/projected-number-autonomous-cars-worldwide/ (accessed 27th January 2022).

Stilgoe, J. (2020). Who's Driving Innovation? Palgrave Macmillan. Switzerland. 74 p. DOI 10.1007/978-3-030-32320-2.

TASS, news-agency. Yandex began testing unmanned vehicles on the Moscow roads. (2019). https://tass.ru/ekonomika/6570313 (accessed 18th July 2020).

Tesla, Inc. (2020). Tesla Press Information. www.tesla.com/en_EU/presskit/autopilot?redirect=no (accessed 18th July 2020).

Tesla, Inc. A Tragic Loss. (2016). www.tesla.com/blog/tragic-loss (accessed 8th May 2020).

TJ. Tesla caught fire and exploded after a collision on the Moscow Ring Road (2019). https://tjournal.ru/news/110821-tesla-zagorelas-i-vzorvalas-posle-stolknoveniya-na-mkade (accessed 8th May 2020).

Yoganandhan, A., Subhashs, S.D., Hebinson, J. & Mohanavel, V. (2020). Fundamentals and development of self-driving cars. Materials today: proceedings. Pp. 1 – 8. DOI: 10.1016/j.matpr.2020.04.736.

Watzenig, D. & Horn, M. (2017). Automated Driving. Springer International Publishing. Switzerland. 620 p. DOI 10.1007/978-3-319-31895-0.

Legal Issues Journal 9(1) 2022: 20–29. © The UK Law and Society Association.

Universality and Particularity: Why Universalism Should be the Standard for Human Rights

Olalekan Moyosore Lalude[1], Nsongurua Udombana[2]

Abstract. The inclination of humans towards self-preservation is the pivot for the universalist notion of human rights and a good starting point of what humans do and desire. What defines good is where the criticism by particularist jurisprudence halts the conclusion of universality. This article aims to resolve the question whether universalism should be the standard for human rights. Using qualitative data analysis, the arguments of the universalists and the particularists on the human rights discourse are examined. A deductive content analysis was applied on a set of data from treaties, declarations, internet sources, and journal articles, arguing that both worldviews failed to address some fundamental issues related to human rights. It is argued that the universality notion of human rights has a better operational value than the particularity perspective, since universality encourages a convergence of purpose which makes for determinable standards within the international law system. The article concludes that the universalist notion of human rights is important to a beneficial agenda of open societies, where governments would be accountable to their

[1]Babcock University School of Law & Security Studies .
Corresponding author: Olalekan Moyosore Lalude,
lalude0368@pg.babcock.edu.ng.
[2]Former Professor of International Law at the Babcock University School of Law & Security Studies.

citizens, and where people would be able to express themselves without fear of oppression.

Keywords: Universality, human rights, particularity, cultural relativism, liberal democracy.

1. Introduction

> All human beings are born free and equal in dignity and rights. They should act towards one another in a spirit of brotherhood. (Universal Declaration of Human Rights, 1948)

Universalism suggests that universal rules, values, or conceptions may be applied to all people and civilizations, regardless of where they are located. These standards are founded on the belief that all individuals are equal, and emphasize human needs, rights, or biological and psychological processes. The Universal Declaration of Human Rights, for example, asserts several rights to all individuals, regardless of culture or nationality, including the ability to marry, own a property, and receive equal protection under the law (Kohfeldt & Grabe, 2014). Universalism is a notion found in the social, political, and physical sciences. The term is, moreover, used in psychology to convey the idea that human experience lies on a spectrum – from fundamental necessities to psychological processes, to core values – that is intrinsic and, hence, identical across persons and cultures. As a result, universalism allows for not just valid cross-cultural comparisons, but also for the development of innovative ideas (Kohfeldt & Grabe, 2014).

On the other hand, particularism has undoubtedly influenced the development of analytical ethics. Its origins may be traced back to Aristotle, who claims that the primary duty of practical knowledge is to identify moral truth by a careful investigation of situational details. On the other hand, the work of Jonathan Dancy carries significance for Particularism's current prominence. He provides a sufficient account of the doctrine's fundamental principles, from a moral metaphysics viewpoint. Despite this, no agreement has been achieved on exactly what particularism entails. It comes in a variety of forms. In general, they all adopt the position that moral principles of some kind play no role in the fundamental fields of ethics. Particularists believe that the distinction between good and wrong is determined by the morally relevant particulars of the issue at hand, rather than by the presence of universal moral principles. Particularists contend that moral principles are, at best, only rules of thumb and, at worst, may lead us into making dangerously wrong decisions. As posited by Tsu (2018), making good moral decisions is the key to success.

Human rights in the meta-narrative of international law have evolved significantly. Human rights have now become a major variable in defining the relations between states. For instance, the offer of foreign aid now comes with human rights as a legislative condition (D'Amato, 1982). This emphasizes the imperative of human rights in the international law system. Before the making of the Universal Declaration of Human Rights (UDHR), human rights matters did not occupy the center stage of international consideration. Before the mid-twentieth century, human rights issues were confined to national jurisdiction until treaties and declarations at the United Nations and by other international organizations highlighted the imperative value of human rights (Schabas, 2021; United Nations Human Rights Office of the High Commissioner, 2021). Human rights were only considered customary international law in the 1960s by scholars (Schabas, 2021). The customary nature of human rights law has been subject to debate. D'Amato argued that some of the public concern for human rights has translated into international law since before 1945, a government would not have been held accountable for the mass murder of its people within its jurisdiction (D'Amato, 1996). D'Amato observed that human rights norms had not received sufficient attention, contrasting the development of human rights and the need to appreciate the universal values that the norms embody. The evolution of human rights in a world that is increasingly cosmopolitan, therefore, has created the need for a re-examination of the age-long debate on the points that universalism and particularism bear for human rights norms.

2. Literature Review

The age-long debate on the appropriate ethical framework for human rights norms has often triggered profound reflections on the nature of human rights and the context of their evolution as norms necessary for social development. These reflections have been situated in different approaches that take into consideration their own experiences, and these experiences define their perspective. One such example is the Third World Approaches to International Law (TWAIL) which, as an intellectual system, is committed through rigorous scholarship to reveal the injustices and inconsistencies of the international law system that works adversely to the interests of the developing world (Appiagyei-Atua, 2015). The experiences that inform TWAIL inspire it towards the conviction that a universalist conception of human rights does nothing but reinforce the imperialism that cloaks international law.

As Appiagyei-Atua (2015) noted, TWAIL as an approach is 'not forthrightly grounded in global ethics perspective (Appiagyei-Atua, 2015).' Examing TWAIL's particularist notions of human rights, its validity stems from the premise that international law must be decolonized. Riegner (2012) has observed that such decolonization presents a challenge to universality and its heterogeneity would imbue the international legal system with its possible higher fragmentation. The danger that TWAIL's blanket approach presents to the universalist conception of human rights is that it derives a context in which human rights in the developing world must be defined such that human rights become open to dangerous interpretations. For instance, the institutionalization of homophobia, which has put the lives of many people from the LGBTQ community at risk and undermined their rights in different parts of Africa, is seen as a needed deviation from the trajectory of human rights consideration in the West (Lalude, 2019). However, Article 2 of the UDHR states that:

Everyone is entitled to all the rights and freedoms outlined in this Declaration, without distinction of any kind, such as race, color, sex, language, religion, political or another opinion, national or social origin, property, birth, or another status. Furthermore, no distinction shall be made based on the political, jurisdictional, or international status of the country or territory to which a person belongs, whether it be independent, trust, non-self-governing, or under any other limitation of sovereignty (Universal Declaration of Human Rights, 1948).

Article 2 of the UDHR has been incorporated in the constitutions of many African states in the form that they prohibit discrimination. The right to freedom from discrimination is even well reflected in

Article 2 of the African Charter on Human and Peoples' Rights (Banjul Charter), yet there is significant discrimination against people of the LGBTQ (Lalude, 2019). A religious perspective offered by the universalist discourse on human rights is that the unity of human purpose presents human life with a dignity that must not be deprived. Vorster (2012) argued that a Christian view would claim that people should not be considered property to be owned, and that they embody a God's image, therefore they are entitled to rights that are God-given and which should inform the protection of their person (Vorster, 2012). In Islam, the conception of rights is framed along with divided opinions (Petersen, 2018). Petersen opined that the Islamic conception of human rights is quite nuanced. For instance, a British Islamic group, Hizb Ut-Tahrir believed that human rights are not a value that is common to all humans. While Abul A'la Mawdudi, a leading Islamist voice in the Mid-20th Century, believed that Islam provided fundamental human rights that were universal such as the right to life, security, freedom, and justice (Petersen, 2018).

The definition of human rights, from the perspective of the United Nations, supports a universalist approach to the discourse of human rights. The meta-narrative of human history from the Second World War has necessitated the universalist approach to human rights since the world had witnessed serious desecrations of humanity for decades. A lesson from the Holocaust was the peak at which it became necessary to chart a new course for a unifying framework for human rights. Before 1948, the cultural relativist approach was the common way in which rights were expressed, as rights were extensions of various associations. Such associations included: family, tribal nation, religious bodies, class, community, or country (University of Minnesota, Human Rights Resource Center, 1993). In the 1930s, when the world had no effective international law framework, through which entities could be held accountable, many African states were still under colonial powers and there was no organization to check what the colonizers did in their territories.

In the United States, there was a mass deportation of Mexican people, including individuals with American citizenship (Timetoast, n.d.). White supremacist groups, like the Ku Klux Klan in 1937, were especially active in the public space (Timetoast, n.d.). Globalization has improved the world's sensitivity to the issue of human rights and further entrenched the universalism of human rights;

such that the issue of the Rohingya Muslims, that were reported to have been attacked by the Myanmar army under the leadership of Aung San Suu Kyi, has become a global issue. There is a relationship between liberal democracy and the globalized perspective on human rights, since both share a universal value. Amartya Sen emphasized the universal value of democracy when he wrote that the spread of democracy in the twentieth century was the most outstanding event of that century. He argued that the universality of the democratic system was novel to the twentieth century. He described how the arguments of earlier political theorists on the suitability of democracy for all states were erroneous in the twentieth century. In addition, Sen prescribed that the suitability of democracy for a state should not be the question, but that democracy should be the standard of measurement of a country's performance (Sen, 1999). The globalized worldview on human rights has gained so much traction especially as democracy became a political fad in the twentieth century. For the universalist conception of human rights, democracy became the political foundation (Sen, 1999). This article would examine the merits of the debate on human rights both as universalist and particularist claims. From the scholarship, it follows that Universalism suggests a standard to measure the success of human rights within societies. Against the open-ended descriptions of human rights that particularism offers.

2. Human Rights, Liberal Democracy and the Notion of Universalism

Universalism is the context that drives a worldview into a systematic mode where a unification occurs with normative practices (Hampden-Turner & Trompenaars, 2002). This supposes that there is no allowance for exceptionalism. Universalism creates a one-dimensional perspective in what is being considered. The advantage that universalism confers on the status of rights is that it makes it easier to outline the expectations from any system, by just measuring it by the common standards. This is the practice today. Furthermore, poor human rights compliance by international organizations in developing states has been considered, and this is true when the metric for evaluation is the universal standard.

Thus, there is a general assumption that human rights are to be complied with, without exceptions.

Universalism makes it easy to define expectations. It allows for a definitive system. One of the enduring merits of the universalist arguments on human rights is that they cause less injury to the cause of human rights by holding a consistent standard to which there must be compliance. The most problematic nature of the universalist notion about human rights is that it is utopian. Another issue with universalism is the condescension with which it treats variance. Anything not conforming to the standard becomes outrightly condemned. Notwithstanding, if there had been improvement, it would only have been noted if there was any room for the fact that human rights develop alongside state politics and the total enlightenment. And so, for states that are developing, human rights regimes certainly should be allowed to develop at their own pace. As Walter argued, there is a neglect of the first and most significant subject in the debate between particularism and universalism, and which is the human being (Walter, 2014). In between both sides of the debate, there is so much effort on the description of the nature of rights that there is a high tendency to forget that human response to the subject of human rights determines the true nature of human rights. The question then remains: what does society think about human rights? The second question focuses more on the sustainability of the universalist approach to human rights at the national level. The conception of human rights in developing states would differ from the notion of human rights in developed states, and this is primarily so since human rights might be better appreciated in states that have high literacy rates, and that have practiced successful democracy.

The consistent fact between liberal democracy and the universalist notion of human rights is the inclusiveness that both systems offer in their worldviews. In the examination of the logic behind the two systems, it was discovered that the reasoning founded in both systems is derived from the commonality and the equality of persons. Firstly, in the consideration of liberal democracy, the emergence of government is based on the equal demonstration of the franchise of willing adult members of a state. In such a system, what confers legality on any government is the demonstration of that inclusive franchise. This is the same way the universalist notion of human rights attempts to give a general description of the notion of human rights. Within this general description, there is no complication in the understanding of human rights. The general description also gives the condition that human rights can only function in a political system that aligns with the universalist notion, since there would be no attempt to prioritize certain rights over others.

The universalist notion of human rights has been critiqued as a cultural insensitivity (Brown, 2000). Brown (2000) argued that the universal notion of human rights was 'cultural imperialism' at its best. He also insisted that the universality which is often ascribed to the human rights system, by the existing international law structures, is pretentious, to the extent that it fails to realize that even within the Western cultural perception of human rights, there is a variance of conceptions (Brown, 2000). He cautioned that the concept of the West is far from the unified concept that it assumes, emphasizing that the Western universal notion of human rights is a West European perspective of human rights (Brown, 2000; Magnarella, 2003). Following this particular clarification on the inconsistency on the inherent cultural framework of the universality of human rights, there are other urgent considerations like the validity of the standards of a universal notion of human rights. How valid are the standards of a culturally appropriated notion of human rights? In approaching this question, the focus should be on what human rights aspire to. A close examination suggests that the universal notion of human rights aspires to the idea that humanity is preserved from itself. Specifically, the safeguards of the universal notion of human rights suggests that human rights attempt to protect the essence of humanity from an individual approach. This is necessary since there is often the risk of the tyranny of the collective.

There is a problem with the philosophical and political underpinnings of the universal notion of human rights. There is often the appearance that the underpinning philosophy of the universal notion of human rights is humanism. Humanism assumes the imperative of humanity: the approach of this assumption has the individual in its focus, and this results from the premise that to estimate the value of the whole of humanity, the individual must be the focus since individual humans make up the collective. This is true, but it raises a question as to the Western system such philosophy justifies. In reflection, to consolidate Brown's argument that the West is an 'analytic construct' (Brown, 2000), the West has come to represent ideas of the Global North, that is, the developed states of the world in the context of developmental discourse. However, the assumption that the universal notion of human rights is a unified Western perspective is incorrect, and it should be noted that the universal notion of human rights is particularly West European (Brown, 2000). Therefore, on this clarification comes the understanding that there are several Western social philosophies, and humanism is just one of such philosophies. Also, the liberal democracy that goes in tow with the universal notion of human rights is as well, West European.

Within East Europe, there is a particularist notion of human rights, and the idea of social democracy frames the human rights system. This follows a medieval history of a diversity of social and political systems. Magnarella (2003) argued that the universal notion of human rights flowed from a system of 'Medieval Christian Thought' (Magnarella, 2003). What this meant was that the philosophical influence on the universalist notion of human rights flowed from both a body of teachings and philosophy that was the heritage of a Western Europe that could not separate church from state. Magnarella, in creating the foundation for the strong criticism of the universalist notion, shows the distinction of the claims of the Universal Declaration of Human Rights 1948, that all humans are the same in 'rights and dignity and the distinct perspective of human rights in Hinduism which allows the conviction that some caste of people is higher than another caste of people. The rights available to the higher caste are not allowed for the lower caste. Magnarella further argued that, just like the reservation of rights is found in Hinduism, so it is found in Islam as well (Magnarella, 2003).

Ilesanmi (2009) observed that the greatest obstacle to the success of the present international human rights regime is culture (Ilesanmi, 2009). What he failed to take into consideration was that religion poses a greater danger, since religion holds even stronger grounds than culture in developing countries. For instance, a Christian sect in Nigeria holds a doctrine that the government must not be criticized. This doctrinal hold is far stronger than any cultural hold on its members. In the Northern part of Nigeria, the observance of the practices of Sunni Islam has suppressed any anthropological peculiarity of the Hausas to the point where the culture has given way to the religion, and therefore religious practices have replaced a larger part of the culture.

Ilesanmi agreed with Magnarella that the universalist notion of human rights took shape through Medieval Christian thought (Ilesanmi, 2009). The presentation of these criticisms, of the universalist notion, does not consider that the very essence of the unified approach was to resolve questions that might weaken the evolution of rights at the international law level, since international law rules attempt to appear operationally distinct from municipal laws. Therefore, it has to function through a set of universal values.

One way to see the justification in the universalist notion is to interrogate its purpose. Human misery through the lens of a particularist demand that human rights must conform to the definition of unique values has heightened in the world today. The universalist notion of human rights for instance would seek to protect stateless persons or undocumented migrants, when under the laws of a state in which they are considered illegal, they might be left vulnerable, and might even be subjected to certain injustices like protracted detention and torture in some circumstances. This is the utmost aim of the universalist notion of human rights that makes it objective.

3. Human Rights and the Particularist Approach

Particularism, as one of the binary 'theories of global order', seeks to explain the context in which human rights should be viewed (Dellavalle, 2010). It provides a set of conditions in which human rights must operate. There is a conservatism argument on the appropriateness of the particularist approach to human rights since it embraces the relativist assumptions that ethical differences of societies influence perceptions of human rights. The conservative criticism of the universalist approach is further underscored by the suggestion that it impairs the practice of pertinent local norms (Movsesian, 2019). Hegelian political philosophy advocates for the centralization of culture (Mullender, Hegel, Human Rights, and Particularism (2003) 30(4), 2003), although whether this refers to a universal approach or a particularist one is unclear. Hegel's position is lost on the arguments from both worldviews on human rights. From this lack of emphasis on either worldview, a third worldview has emerged, that distinguishes itself by not prescribing either of the worldviews but advocates for consideration of cultural peculiarities and the importance of human rights.

This third approach refuses to take a clear position on what might be crucial to policy considerations related to human rights. However, the danger of not taking a clear position is that it creates a vacuum of philosophical direction for policy, such that there is allowance to prioritize either the dictates of tradition or the entreaties of human rights. For instance, in Saudi Arabia, society allows for the discrimination and the abuse of women through a system known as the male guardianship system (Human Rights Watch, 2019). This system subjects women to the care of a man, who might be a father, brother, or husband, and who is expected to make crucial decisions for her. The country treats women as 'permanent legal minors' (Human Rights Watch, 2019). The Hegelian position does not prescribe what should take precedence in such instances. Many times, there have been collisions between those who claim there are gross violations of human rights in the Middle East and those, which include the leadership of states in the Middle East, who believe the system should be left the way it is. From the Middle Eastern example of women's freedom and rights being denied, it has often been that human rights violations that are gender-driven are often explained away and excused with the particularist argument that social traditions are important in the implementation of human rights (Lakatos, 2018).

The particularist approach, leaning on an ethical relativist morality, believes cultures and tradition determine how society would implement human rights. There is a high distinction between the merits of particularism in its view of human rights and the end it achieves. This distinction comes from the point that particularism tries to describe the systematic deviation from the simplistic prescription of the universalist approach. Particularism attempts a realistic conceptualization of the problem of implementing human rights in social systems where particular practices might work against the agenda of the contemporary regime of human rights.

The end that particularism achieves is unintentional. It concludes that societies have the liberty of selecting the human rights that suits them. The problem with this conclusion is that human rights would never develop if their progress were to be encumbered by such an end. Lakatos has argued that particularism has been used many times to defend totalitarian regimes (Lakatos,

2018). This is also the case in Africa when totalitarian regimes tried fighting the spread of liberal democracy on the continent, by attending to protests with deadly force.

The cultural and ethical relativism that powers the argument of particularism emphasizes the understanding of a people. The logic seems to be that people cannot be better than their culture, as culture is viewed as a factor that shapes social thought. In this respect, people cannot be better than their religion, because, over time, they may begin to think alongside the claims of their doctrinal teachings.

The variance of the particularist approach could be seen from two subsets to wit: the cultural and the ethical. Religion would be assumed to be ethical since it usually advances a moral system of teachings. Cultural relativism could progress from the point of political practices to become something much more concrete, especially when these political practices are the pillar of state ideologies. This was the case with former socialist states. The Union of Soviet Socialist Republics was a police state and it repressed negative opinions of the state with force, such that writers and artists began to seek asylum in the United States where there was freedom of expression.

This bears resemblance with Chinese political history and the political practices of Red China still influence the social culture of modern-day China. The danger in the particularist conception of human rights is expressed in the fact that when political culture becomes crucial in the approach to the implementation of human rights, then human rights might never be realized in their full potentials to secure societies from different forms of tyranny. An instance is the militarization of socialism which, over time, has made the political system quite insensitive to the full expression of human rights.

For instance, the attempts in Africa at indigenizing human rights by the creation of the treaties; African Charter on Human and Peoples' Rights (1982), The African Charter on the Rights and Welfare of the Child, The Protocol to the African Charter of Human and Peoples' Rights on the Rights of Women in Africa, are particularist, just like other regional attempts at creating a cultural context for the interpretation of human rights. Therefore, since the African philosophy of human rights is communitarian, it was necessary to contextualize human rights in that philosophical system (Lalude, 2019). Douzinas (2002) argued while using the Hegelian perspective as a theoretical framework that the peculiarities of individuality are important to the adequate protection of human rights (Mullender, 2003). He further stressed the importance of the individual peculiarities as being imperative to the legal recognition of human rights (Douzinas, 2002; Douzinas, 2000).

The Douzinas approach seems even more peculiar, as it focuses on the individual rather than whole cultures. In defending the relativist conception of different cultures of human rights, it is important to regard that it is easy to disguise mischievous non-compliance with the argument of cultural relativity of the moral values that guide the consciousness of human rights in different cultures. The Permanent Representative of Iran to the United Nations in 1984, expressed that the Universal Declaration of Human Rights "did not accord with the system of values recognized by the Islamic Republic of Iran" and "his country would therefore not hesitate to violate its prescriptions" (Lakatos, 2018; Burke, 2011). It would be recalled that Iran and many other Middle Eastern countries are not free societies. In 2019, Human Rights Watch reported a critical state of human rights in Iran. The organization reported how the state had continually violated the right of peaceful assembly and free expression when it targeted protesters (Human Rights Watch, 2018). The statist arrangement that invested so much power in the socialist states during the times of the Iron Curtain, is the same arrangement that characterizes a Middle Eastern state like Iran.

Transacting human rights from a statist height allows for a huge imbalance in the power relations between the people and the state. Human rights are supposed to be the vehicle through which common people express the power of their political collective as it is demonstrated in liberal democracy. The legal mandate of a political collective that concretizes the legitimacy of any government is the recognition and the acceptance of the expressive power of the political collective of a people. It could be argued that the universality which defines the international human rights regime draws on the commonalities of people from all cultures, religions, and political convictions. Additionally, universal values within human communities, such as the right to life, tend to the preservation of humanity. Arguably, that since all human beings have emotions, then all humans have certain things in common. However, not all humans necessarily react fabourably to liberty.

In the United States, Wall Street Journal conducted a poll in 2019, on prospects for the liberal Democrat party in 2020. It was found that an American majority supported the idea of 'anyone buying into Medicare' (McCormick, 2019). The difference between the majority that supported that scheme and the other was just six percent (McCormick, 2019). What this meant was that the idea of security is held higher than freedom (Lemieux, 2019). The idea that liberty is not a universal value, that some people feel secure under despotic authority has been favored by Buchanan when he expressed the idea that, 'The thirst or desire for freedom, and responsibility, is perhaps not nearly so universal as so many post-Enlightenment philosophers have assumed (Buchanan, 2005).'

The idea of the non-universality of liberty has been one of the solid pillars of the particularist claims. This then puts a question to the purpose of universalist human rights, what is the value of human rights with a universalist nature? History has shown that human preferences could be destructive; from populist ideas that were tested in the public space and were discovered to resonate with the resentment of diversity by the common people, who thought that foreigners steal jobs. If human rights were to be argued from the perspective that liberty is not as universal as it was once thought, then it would mean that human rights should be judged from the subjectivity of human preference. The risk in this is that human rights become deemphasized in themselves, and this puts political, cultural, and civilizational development in jeopardy.

4. Conclusion

The universalist and particularist debate on human rights has often exposed the aspiration of human rights in the world. The universalist notion of human rights appears to be culturally imperialistic, even though it furthers the idea that human societies should be free and should support individual liberties. This idea of individual liberties has been interrogated by particularist arguments that individual liberties cannot be determined by mere assumptions of what they should be. This is valid and a fine point for consideration. However, the danger in the particularist arguments is that it leaves many ends open for contextualization. It could also aid the rogue intentions of states with despotic governments in the repression of their people. The importance of the universalist notion of human rights is that they open societies to the possibilities of a cosmopolitan existence, which enhances culture and overall human development.

References

Sen, A. (1999). Democracy as a Universal Value. *Journal of Democracy, 10*(3), 3-17. Retrieved from https://www.unicef.org/socialpolicy/files/Democracy_as_a_Universal_Value.pdf

Appiagyei-Atua, K. (2015). Ethical dimensions of Third World Approaches to International Law. *African Journal of Legal Studies, 8*(3-4).

Brown, C. (2000). Universal Human Rights? An Analysis of the Human-Rights Culture' and its Critics. In R. G. Patman, *Universal Human Rights.* New York: St. Martin's Press .

Buchanan, J. M. (2005). Afraid to Be Free: Dependency as Desideratum . *Policy Challenges and Political Responses: Public Choice Perspectives on the Post-9/11 World, 124*(1/2), 19-13.

Burke, R. (2011). *Decolonization and the Evolution of International Human Rights .* University of Pennsylvania Press .

D'Amato, A. (1996). Human Rights as Part of Customary International Law: A Plea for Change of Paradigms. *Georgia Journal of International & Comparative Law, Fall,1995 /Winter.*

D'Amato, A. (1982). The Concept of Human Rights in International Law*. *Columbia Law Review, 86*(6).

Dellavalle, S. (2010). Beyond Particularism: Remarks on Some Recent Approaches to the Idea of a Universal Political and Legal Order. *European Journal of International Law, 21*(3), 765-788.

Douzinas, C. (2000). *The End of Human Rights: Critical Thought at the Turn of the Century'.* Bloomsbury Academic .

Douzinas, C. (2002). Identity, Recognition, Rights or What Can Hegel Teach Us About Human Rights? . *Journal of Law & Society, 29*, 379.

Hampden-Turner, C., & Trompenaars, F. (2002). *Building Cross-Cultural Competence: How to Create Wealth from Conflicting Values* . New Haven & London: Yale University Press.

Human Rights Watch. (2018). *Iran: Events of 2018.* Retrieved from Human Rights Watch: https://www.hrw.org/world-report/2019/country-chapters/iran

Human Rights Watch. (2019, January 30). *Saudi Arabia: 10 Reasons Why Women Flee* . Retrieved from Human Rights Watch: https://www.hrw.org/news/2019/01/30/saudi-arabia-10-reasons-why-women-flee

Ilesanmi, S. O. (2009, November 4). Universalism and Relativism in Human Rights Debate in Africa: A Critique of Cultural Essentialism .

Kohfeldt, D., & Grabe, S. (2014). Universalism. *Encyclopedia of Critical Psychology.* (T. Teo, Ed.) Springer Link. Retrieved from https://link.springer.com/referenceworkentry/10.1007%2F978-1-4614-5583-7_545

Lakatos, I. (2018). Thoughts on Universalism versus Cultural Relativism, with Special Attention to Women's Rights. *Pécs Journal of Internattional and European Law, 2018*(1), 6-25.

Lalude, O. M. (2019). The African Moral Perspectives on Human Rights. *Interrnational Journal of Legal Studies and Research, 8*(2), 205-222.

Lemieux, P. (2019, October, 7). *Do People Want to Be Free* . Retrieved from The Library of Economics and Liberty: https://www.econlib.org/do-people-want-to-be-free/

Magnarella, P. J. (2003). Questioning the Universality of Human Rights. *Human Rights and Welfare, 3*(1), 16.

McCormick, J. (2019, September 22). *U.S. Voters Support Expanding Medicare but Not Eliminating Private Health Insurance* . Retrieved from The Wall Street Journal: https://www.wsj.com/articles/u-s-voters-support-expanding-medicare-but-not-eliminating-private-health-insurance-11569157204

Movsesian, M. (2019, August 16). *Human Rights Anti-Universalism —From the Left.* (St. John's Law School Center for Law and Religion Law and Religion Forum) Retrieved from Law and Religion Forum: https://lawandreligionforum.org/2019/08/16/human-rights-particularism-from-the-left/

Mullender, R. (2003). Hegel, Human Rights, and Particularism . *Journal of Law and Society, 30*(4), 554-574.

Mullender, R. (2003). Hegel, Human Rights, and Particularism (2003) 30(4). *Journal of Law and Society, 30*(4), 554-574.

Petersen, M. J. (2018, June 11). *Islam and human rrights: clash or compatibility.* Retrieved from LSE: https://blogs.lse.ac.uk/religionglobalsociety/2018/06/islam-and-human-rights-clash-or-compatibility/

Riegner, M. (2012). How universal are international law and development? Engaging with postcolonial and Third World scholarship from the perspective of its other*. *Verfassung und Recht in Übersee / Law and Politics in Africa, Asia and Latin, 45*(2).

Schabas, W. A. (2021). *The Customary International Law of Human Rights.* Oxford Scholarship Online.

Timetoast. (n.d.). *1930s Human Rights Issues Timeline.* Retrieved from Timetoast: https://www.timetoast.com/timelines/1910-civil-rights-timeline

Tsu, P. S.-H. (2018, March 28). *Particularism in Ethics.* Retrieved from Oxford Bibliographies: https://www.oxfordbibliographies.-com/view/document/obo-9780195396577/obo-9780195396577-0367.xml

United Nations Human Rights Office of the High Commissioner. (2021). *International Human Rights Law.* Retrieved November 8, 2021, from United Nations Human Rights Office of the High Commissioner: https://www.ohchr.org/en/professionalinterest/pages/internationallaw.aspx

Universal Declaration of Human Rights. (1948). Article 1.

Universal Declaration of Human Rights. (1948).

University of Minnesota, Human Rights Resource Center. (1993). *A Short History of Human Rights' adapted from David Shiman, Teaching Human Rights,.* Retrieved from University of Minnesota, Human Rights Resource Center: hrlibrary.umn.edu/edumat/hreduseries/hereandnow/Part-1/short-history.htm

Vorster, N. (2012). A theological perspective on human dignity, equality and freedom. *Verbum et Ecclesia, 33*(1).

Walter, L. (2014). Theories of Universal Human Rights and the Individual's Perspective. *Politikon the IAPSS Journal of Political Science, 25.*

Management of Protected Areas in Albania Toward European Standards

Dr. Stela Meçaj[1], Dr. Jonida Mehmetaj[2]

Abstract. Albania has established a representative system of protected areas, covering almost 16% of the Albanian territory. Over the past 20 years, protected areas in Albania have not been integrated into national and local development policies. Most of the natural resources in Albania are under the threat of constant pressures such as illegal logging, hunting, fishing. The National Agency for Protected Areas is actively working to improve the management of protected areas according to the requirements, international standards, and experience of other European countries. In the field of nature conservation and biodiversity, Albania has an obligation to identify and protect natural heritage areas of high conservation interest for the European Union. Using qualitative research methodology, this paper aims to address the issues related to protected areas by also identifying the measures that may improve their management. The findings from the analysis highlight problems and delays in meeting Albania's obligations under the integration process in the field of nature conservation and biodiversity.

Keywords: protected areas, natural resources, national park, natural landscape, Natura 2000

---

[1]University "Ismail Qemali" Vlora, Albania. Corresponding author: Dr. Stela Meçaj, stela.mecaj@univlora.edu.al.
[2]University "Ismail Qemali" Vlora, Albania.

Introduction

According to the definition of IUCN, a protected area is *"A clearly defined geographical space, recognised, dedicated and managed, through legal or other effective means, to achieve the long-term conservation of nature with associated ecosystem services and cultural values".*[3] They have cultural, historical, archaeological, and cultural heritage, which was given a certain status by law for their protection and development. The earliest types of protected areas for the conservation of resources can be traced back to around 200 BC and protected areas were opened or created for public recreational use.[4] In Albania, the stationary conservation of nature and biodiversity has only begun to develop in the last 50 years, and especially after the 90s of the last century.[5] The sites designated as protected areas receive international attention, such as financial institutions, including the European Investment Bank[6], the European Bank for Reconstruction and Development[7], World Bank[8] etc. Establishing protected areas is a key strategy for protecting biological resources.[9] The primary goal of protected ar-

[3]N. Dudley, (Ed.), Guidelines for Applying Protected Area Management Categories. (IUCN, 2008).

[4]S. Chape, M. D. Spalding & M. D. Jenkins, The World's Protected Areas: Status, Values and Prospects in the 21st Century. 376 pp. (University of California Press, 2008).

[5]Sektori i Silvikulturës, Drejtoria e Pyjeve Agjencia Kombëtare e Mjedisit, Zonat e mbrojtura, historia, gjendja dhe monitorimi, 14.04.2014, fq. 2.

[6]European Investment Bank. Environmental and Social Handbook. (2013).

[7]European Bank for Reconstruction and Development. Environmental and Social Policy. (2014).

[8]The World Bank. World Bank Operational Manual. Revised Version 2013. OP 4.04 Natural habitats (2013).

[9]Ma Ben, Zhang Yuqian, Hou Yilei and Wen Yali, Do Protected Areas Matter? A Systematic Review of the Social and Ecological Impacts of the Establishment of Protected Areas, International Journal of Environmental Research and Public Health, 2020, pg. 1.

eas is to conserve biodiversity.[10] The establishment of protected areas has been frequently reported as having negative impact on local people[11], but also, there are significant positive livelihood effects found in many places.[12] In all countries, laws, policies, incentives and legal frameworks affect the establishment, management and effectiveness of protected areas.[13] As the global agenda for protected areas evolves and changes, so too must the policies that guide the establishment, planning, resource use and management of protected areas must be created or modified in order to meet these changing expectations.[14] Many studies suggest climate change could wreak havoc on major life support systems.[15] These impacts are very likely to compromise the potential of hydrological systems to purify water, process contaminants, control

---

[10]UNEP-WCMC, IUCN, NGS. Protected Planet Report 2018; UNEP-WCMC, IUCN and NGS: Cambridge, UK; Gland, Switzerland; Washington, DC, USA, 2018. FAO, UNEP. The State of the World's Forests 2020. Forests, Biodiversity and People; FAO: Rome, Italy, 2020; Available online: https://doi.org/10.4060/ca8642en (accessed on 27 September 2020).

[11]B. Ma; Z. Zhao, H. Ding; Y. Wen, Household costs and benefits of biodiversity conservation: Case study of Sichuan giant panda reserves in China. Environ. Dev. Sustain. 2018, 20, 1665–1686. H. Yang, F. Lupi, J. Zhang, X. Chen, J. Liu, Feedback of telecoupling: The case of a payments for ecosystem services program. Ecol. Soc. 2018, 23, 45.

[12]P. J. Ferraro, M. M. Hanauer, D. A. Miteva, J. L Nelson, S. K Pattanayak, C. Nolte, K. R. Sims, Estimating the impacts of conservation on ecosystem services and poverty by integrating modeling and evaluation. Proc. Natl. Acad. Sci. USA 2015, 112, 7420–7425. M. D. Pour, N. Motiee, A. A. Barati, F. Taheri, H. Azadi, K. Gebrehiwot, F. Witlox, Impacts of the Hara biosphere reserve on livelihood and welfare in Persian Gulf. Ecol. Econ. 2017, 141, 76–86.

[13]Protected Areas for the 21st Century: Lessons from UNDP/GEF's Portofolio, pg. 17.

[14]Ibid.

[15]M. L. Parry, O. F. Canziani, J. P. Palutikof, P. J. van der Linden and C. E. Hanson, eds. (2007); Contribution of Working Group II to the Fourth Assessment Report of the Intergovernmental Panel on Climate Change. Cambridge: Cambridge University Press.

floods, supply water, sequester carbon and nitrogen, regulate temperatures, and provide erosion and soil control.[16]

However, the creation of potential connections between existing protected areas, added to their surfaces as one of the major network targets Natura 2000, as well as taking appropriate measures for the management and conservation of nature require the establishment of a clear management mechanism and specific to treating them. This gave rise to the necessity of secession from existing administrations and the creation of a proper management structure fully dedicated to these areas.[17] Traditionally, protected area restoration has focused on improving the overall condition of degraded habitats. Restoration activities include, for example, prescribed burning, removal of invasive species, reintroduction of top predators and other key species, barrier removal (such as fencing and dams), and afforestation on deforested lands.[18] Countries have developed regional networks and established large, contiguous protected areas primarily for the purpose of creating core habitat for wide-ranging species, and for protecting biological sources that can replenish surrounding areas.[19] In addition, efforts to support and encourage the creation of transboundary protected areas have largely focused on the promotion of peace and harmonious international relations and reducing conflicts between

[16]M. A Palmer, D. P. Lettenmaier, N. L. Poff, S. L. Postel, B. Richter and R. Warner (2010); Climate change and river ecosystems: protection and adaptation options. Environmental Management 44: 1053-1068.

[17]Botim periodik i Qendrës Rajonale të Mjedisit (REC) - Shqipëri, Mjedisi Sot, Nr. 150, 2016, fq. 9.

[18]National Parks Directorate (2009); Principles and Guidelines for Ecological Restoration in Canada's Protected Natural Areas. Gatineau, Ontario: National Parks Directorate.

[19]K. R Crooks and M. Sanjayan, eds. (2006); Connectivity Conservation. Cambridge: Cambridge University Press; Bennett, A.F. (2003); Linkages in the Landscape: The Role of Corridors and Connectivity in Wildlife Conservation. Gland, Switzerland: IUCN; and G. L Worboys, W.L. Francis and M. Lockwood (2010); Connectivity Conservation Management: A Global Guide. London: Earthscan.

countries.[20] Recent studies show that large regional networks and transboundary protected areas are critical in enabling climate adaptation at large scales,[21] maintaining overall landscape resilience,[22] maintaining ecosystem services,[23] and enhancing local livelihoods.[24]

The Protected Area can be a forest, a lagoon, a valuable agricultural land, an alpine area, a marine and coastal area, or many other types of natural or partially modified ecosystems, as well as any combination of different types of ecosystems. The Protected Areas are divided into six categories, defined by their management objectives, such as: Strict Nature Reserves/Science Reserves (category I); National Parks (category II); Nature Monuments (category III); Managed Nature Reserves (category IV); Protected Landscape Areas (category V); Managed Nature Reserves (category VI).[25] Protected areas contribute to sustainable development through: protection of highly sensitive species by

---

[20]L. Braack, T. Sandwith, D. Peddle, D. and T. Petermann (2006); Security Considerations in the Planning and Management of Transboundary Conservation Areas. Gland, Switzerland: IUCN, Gland, Switzerland; and Sandwith, T., C. Shine, L. Hamilton and D. Sheppard (2001); Transboundary Protected Areas for Peace and Co-operation. Gland, Switzerland: IUCN.

[21]I. Thompson, B. Mackey, S. McNulty and A. Mosseler (2009); Forest Resilience, Biodiversity, and Climate Change. A synthesis of the Biodiversity/Resilience/Stability Relationship in Forest Ecosystems. Technical Series No. 43. Montreal: Secretariat of the CBD.

[22]C. Carroll, J. R. Dunk and A. Moilanen (2010); Optimizing Resiliency of Reserve Networks to Climate Change: Multispecies Conservation Planning in the Pacific Northwest, USA. Global Change Biology, 16(3): 891-904.

[23]C. Groves, M. Anderson, C. Enquist, E. Girvet, T. Sandwith, L. Schwarz and R. Shaw (2010); Climate Change and Conservation: A Primer for Assessing Impacts and Advancing Ecosystem Based Adaptation in The Nature Conservancy. Arlington, VA: TNC. 59 pp.

[24]S. Hagerman, H. Dowlatabadi, T. Satterfield, T. McDaniels (2010); Expert views on biodiversity conservation in an era of climate change. Global Environmental Change Part A: Human & Policy Dimensions, 20(1): 192-207.

[25]Sektori i Silvikulturës, Drejtoria e Pyjeve Agjencia Kombëtare e Mjedisit, Zonat e mbrojtura, historia, gjendja dhe monitorimi, 14.04.2014, fq. 3-4.

humans; conservation of natural vegetation on lands with low productivity; protection of water reserves and land in eroded areas; regulating and purifying water flow; protection of forests and wetlands; protecting people from natural disasters, such as floods and landslides; maintaining natural genetic resources relevant to medicine or racial improvements; maintaining critical habitats for the feeding, reproduction or recreation of species used; providing income and jobs from tourism development.[26]

Research Methodology

This paper uses a qualitative research methodology which includes logical deductions based on historical facts. The reasoning process used in qualitative research perceptually involves assembling individual pieces to create the whole. Qualitative research methodology includes a broad understanding of human behavior and the reasons that direct that behavior. This paper includes secondary sources for data collection. The secondary source includes the collection of data through books, articles, newspapers, magazines, authentic websites, etc. The methods used are descriptive, comparative, and analytical.

The paper addressed two scientific research questions:

1. Has Albania fulfilled its commitments to protect protected areas in accordance with European standards?
2. What are the measures to improve the situation in this environmental sector?
3. Albanian legal framework for protected areas in the approach to European legislation

Albania has its own environmental legislation in the field of nature protection, which is generally aligned with EU standards. The process of accession of the Republic of Albania to international environmental conventions and protocols began in the 1990s. Conventions are already integrated into the whole set of activities undertaken by environmental authorities. Commitments to adhere

[26]Ibid, fq. 3.

to international environmental documents, on the one hand, significantly increased the number of conventions and protocols to which Albania was party, while on the other hand, problems of their implementation were identified.[27] Some of the most important conventions that determine the importance of protected areas are: the Convention on Biological Diversity; Berne Convention for the Conservation of Wild Flora and Fauna; CITES Convention on International Trade in Endangered Species; Ramsar Convention on Wetlands; Landscape Convention etc.

The Convention on Biological Diversity gives parties the right to use and manage information in the field of biodiversity. This convention provides for an important role of protected areas in national and international plans for biodiversity, defining the importance of the creation of the network of protected areas.[28] The Network of Protected Areas constitutes a strong basis, through the promotion of identification, for the protection and preservation of cultural and natural heritage throughout the world. Pursuant to the obligations of the Convention on Biological Diversity, by Decision of the Council of Ministers no. 31, dated 21.1.2016 was adopted the "Strategic Policy Document for Biodiversity Protection" and the action plan until 2020. The Strategic Policy Document for Biodiversity Protection clearly identifies the main areas of work, namely: the increase of the Protected area, drafting of Management Plans and their implementation; complementing the EU-wide legal framework for nature and the environment; eliminating illegal logging and hunting, implementing the legal framework as well as capacity building activities and implementing action plans for endangered species and habitats.[29]

The Convention "On the conservation of wild flora and fauna and the natural environment in Europe" (Bern) was ratified by Albania on 02.03.1998 and aims to guarantee the conservation of wild flora and fauna and their natural habitats.[30] Ecosystems, habitats, floristic and faunistic species are under constant and sus-

---

[27]Instituti për Ruajtjen e Natyrës në Shqipëri, Legjislacioni bazë dhe mbështetës mjedisor për menaxhimin e zonave të mbrojtura, 2017, fq. 12.

[28]Konventa e Diversitetit Biologjik, ratifikuar më 05.01.1994.

[29]Dokumenti i politikave strategjike për mbrojtjen e biodiversitetit, 2015, fq. 7.

[30]Fletore Zyrtare nr. 7, datë 04.04.1998.

tained pressure on human activities, and their qualities are being destroyed, due to inadequate management.[31] To prevent these occurrences, states have created protected area systems by increasing investment in contemporary management not only locally but also regionally and beyond.[32]

Albania has signed the Law no. 9021, dated 6.3.2003 "On the accession of the Republic of Albania to the Convention on International Trade in Endangered Species of Wild Flora and Fauna"[33]. According to this convention, member states are obliged to implement its obligations and relevant annexes. These appendices include all endangered species that are or could be affected by trade. Trading members of these species must be subject to particularly strict regulation to prevent further risk to their lives and should only be allowed in exceptional cases[34].

On March 26, 1996, Albania became a party to the Ramsar Convention, which is the Convention of Wetlands of international importance, mainly for wetlands of waterfowl. Wetlands are one of the most productive environments in the world; they are also called the "cradle" of biological diversity, providing water and primary productivity for the existence of countless species of mammalian plants, birds, reptiles, aquifers, fish, and invertebrate species[35]. Signing must also fulfill certain obligations, such as: designating a wetland to be included in the list of wetlands of international importance; taking measures for their good management, and consequently the conservation of species, especially waterfowl. The Ramsar Convention has as its main objective promotes shared responsibility of signatory countries to the protection of wetlands, which are important for water birds, who are perma-

---

[31]Instituti për Ruajtjen e Natyrës në Shqipëri, Legjislacioni bazë dhe mbështetës mjedisor për menaxhimin e zonave të mbrojtura, 2017, fq. 17.

[32]Instituti për Ruajtjen e Natyrës në Shqipëri, Legjislacioni bazë dhe mbështetës mjedisor për menaxhimin e zonave të mbrojtura, 2017, fq. 17.

[33]Fletore Zyrtare nr. 22, datë 2.4.2003, fq. 665.

[34]Konventa "Për tregtinë ndërkombëtare të llojeve të rrezikuara të florës dhe faunës së egër" (CITES), 22.06.1979.

[35]Konventa e Ramsarit. Aksesuar ne adresën e internetit www.ammk-rks.net/repository/docs/2_Shkurti-Dita_Nderkombetare_e_Ligatinave-Broshura.pdf, datë 07.08.2019.

nent residents of the wetlands, and what may also be promote "smart use" of wet ecosystems.[36] The implementation of these responsibilities is being realized in the ecosystems included in the list of wetlands of international importance, especially as waterfowl habitats.

By Law no. 87/2016, dated 8.9.2016 Albania adheres to the European Landscape Convention.[37] The main objective to be achieved is to promote and promote the protection, management and planning of landscapes, to organize cross-border, regional and European co-operation as an important element for the quality of life of the population in urban and rural environments, in the areas of environment, in degraded areas, in those unaffected by defining objectives for quality growth of landscapes[38].The Convention also relates to informality in the development of land, territory, urban and rural areas and creates an institutional, economic and social environment for the sustainable development of the territory.

As part of integrating Albania into the European Union, in the field of environmental protection and respectively in terms of nature conservation, partial harmonization with the European Birds and Habitats Directives has been achieved.[39] Concerning the approximation of nature conservation and biodiversity legislation, the Strategic Policy Paper on Biodiversity Conservation reports that Albania has made an estimated progress of 85%. Prohibition of hunting showed progress in protecting the fauna, extending the detention period by another 5 years. The Albanian Parliament approved a 10-year moratorium on the use of forest wood for business purposes. Regulations on timber and law enforcement on forestry, administration and trade still need to be approximated. Progress has been made in strengthening inspection capacity.[40]

Further, in January 2017, the new Law on Protected Areas no. 81/2017 was adopted, which represents the widespread harmoni-

---

[36]Konventa e ligatinave të rëndësisë ndërkombëtare, veçanërisht si habitat i shpendëve të ujit (Ramsarit), 1971.

[37]Fletore Zyrtare Nr. 117, fq. 2605.

[38]Konventa Evropiane e Peisazhit, 20.10.2000.

[39]EU Policy Hub, Ruajtja e natyrës dhe rëndësia e saj në procesin e integrimit, Hub Monitor, Issue Brief 30.11.2017, fq. 3.

[40]Instituti për Ruajtjen e Natyrës në Shqipëri, Legjislacioni bazë dhe mbështetës mjedisor për menaxhimin e zonave të mbrojtura, 2017, fq. 21-22.

sation of national biodiversity conservation legislation with that of the EU. This law is devoted to a special section (namely section V) of protected areas of international interest and in particular Natura 2000 areas.[41] The implementation of the Natura 2000 process requires the assessment of the entire territory of the country and not the concentration of work only on the National Network of Protected Areas. Implementation of the appropriate approach would enable the identification of areas of high conservation interest for the European Union, based on the Birds and Habitats Directives[42]. The Natura 2000 process represents one of the greatest achievements the country can make in the field of nature conservation and sustainable management and biodiversity.

By identifying and approving the list of possible areas Natura 2000 implementing the commitments of the integration process, effective protection still must be guaranteed. Moreover, investments in hydropower plants must comply with the nature of protection obligations[43]. The capacities and financial instruments for the National Agency of Protected Areas remain very limited, with the law prohibiting its financial autonomy. Law enforcement should be guaranteed in the event of deforestation and logging, and culprits should be prosecuted. Investments in hydropower plants must comply with national and international environmental protection obligations[44].

Problems of management of conservation areas of special interest in Albania

In order to gain status as a conservation area of special interest, the area must meet at least one of the following criteria: a) have a

[41]EU Policy Hub, Ruajtja e natyrës dhe rëndësia e saj në procesin e integrimit, Hub Monitor, Issue Brief 30.11.2017, fq. 3.

[42]Ibid, fq. 4.

[43]Komisioni Evropian, Dokument Pune i Stafit të Komisionit, Raporti i Progresit të Shqipërisë për vitin 2018, Bruksel 17.4.2018 SWD (2018) 151 final, fq. 87.

[44]Komisioni Evropian, Dokument Pune i Stafit të Komisionit, Raporti i Progresit të Shqipërisë për vitin 2019, Bruksel, 29.5.2019 SWD (2019) 215 final, fq. 90-91.

high diversity of species and/or habitats; b) have a low density of species and/or habitats; c) have representation; d) have a critical minimum ecosystem size; e) have naturalness, inheritance and integrity; f) have scientific value; g) be characterized by ecological vulnerability/vulnerable species; h) be characterized by non-repetitive/endemic species; i) there is a high risk of being threatened by interference with human activities; j) can provide opportunities for wildlife conservation.[45] Special attention has been paid to the risks to the country's biodiversity and the obstacles and deficiencies in its monitoring, conservation and management.[46]

In natural diversity of our country, especially in the protected areas, the terrestrial and aquatic ecosystems, floristic and faunistic species, which extend from the marine-coastal belt to the hilly and hilly belt and deeper into the high mountains, are prominent. Such an extension is contained in the network of areas of the country, as a very important instrument for in situ conservation of nature and biodiversity, protection, and sustainable development of bionatural resources. National Parks comprise the majority of Protected Areas, where forests occupy the major importance as the most important area of high biodiversity expression.[47]

The Natura 2000 Area Network is a joint contribution of European Union member states to fulfill the obligations deriving from the Berne Convention. The Emerald Network includes Special Conservation Interest Areas identified in countries that have ratified the "Convention on the Conservation of Europe's Wild Fauna and Wildlife" or otherwise known as the "Bern Convention"[48]. Areas of the Emerald Network receive special attention only when all or part of their surface is simultaneously within the boundaries of the National Network of Protected Areas, while the surface of the

---

[45]Neni 11 i Ligjit Nr. 81/2017 Për zonat e mbrojtura. Ky ligj është përafruar pjesërisht me Direktivën e Këshillit 92/43/KEE, datë 21 maj 1992, "Për ruajtjen e habitateve natyrore dhe të florës dhe faunës së egër", të ndryshuar", Numri CELEX 31992L0043, Fletorja Zyrtare e Bashkimit Europian, Seria L, nr. 206, datë 22.7.1992, fq. 7- 50.

[46]Sektori i Silvikulturës, Drejtoria e Pyjeve Agjencia Kombëtare e Mjedisit, Zonat e mbrojtura, historia, gjendja dhe monitorimi, 14.04.2014, fq. 4.

[47]Ibid, fq. 7.

[48]EU Policy Hub, Ruajtja e natyrës dhe rëndësia e saj në procesin e integrimit, Hub Monitor, Issue Brief 30.11.2017, fq. 5.

Emerald Network extends outside The Protected Areas Network is treated as any ordinary part of the territory.[49]In many cases these areas are threatened by a large number of environmental problems, such as: hunting; cutting of forest areas; fires; water and landscape pollution; construction of hydropower plants and other facilities. These activities have caused degradation of natural habitats and loss of biodiversity in the Emerald areas, including species of high conservation interest for the European Union.

The aforementioned activities may be illegal as well as lawful. Generally, for illegal activities there is a reported willingness to control them, presenting concrete measures and comparative statistics of estimating the intensity of the phenomenon from year to year. In some cases, inappropriate development or investment plans have been introduced in certain areas of the Emerald Network. Legislating and permitting plans or projects of this nature, which consist of the alienation of significant natural areas within the Emerald Zones and consequently the threat of habitats and species, constitutes an open violation of European Union rules and standards for the conservation and management of these zones.[50] Presentation of urbanization plans of some of the best areas, a symbol of Albanian nature, such as the case of the Vjosa-Narta Protected Landscape and the recent case of Divjaka-Karavasta National Park that best illustrates this claim.[51] Divjaka-Karavasta National Park is the symbol of Albanian nature and the most important wetland for birds in the southern Adriatic. This area is the habitat for more than 245 bird species and represents the area with the highest faunistic diversity in the country.[52]

In Albania, the national network of protected areas covers 18% of the territory. Albania is progressing towards meeting the conditions for opening negotiations on the chapter on environment and climate change. At the same time the creation of the National Agency of Protected Areas around 100 people from the agency and regional offices have been trained in the protection of biodiversity, implementation plans and monitoring protocols, fighting fires and natural disasters, as well as participated in study visits and conferences at home and abroad.Part of the progress is the

[49]Ibid, fq. 6.
[50]Ibid, fq. 7.
[51]Ibid, fq. 6.
[52]Ibid.

creation of the National Biodiversity Database and the Wildlife Management and Information System which are used to collect and analyze wildlife data and biodiversity status in Albania.[53] In the context of identifying potential Natura 2000 sites a preliminary list of 43 areas has been proposed. Experts point out that the only way to create a sustainable and competitive economy is to protect nature and create a balance between human resources and ambitions related to how we want to live.[54]

Conclusions

Albanian legislation has been substantially aligned with the main principles and standards of the European Union, but these principles have not been sufficiently elaborated and adapted to better meet the needs of regulating Albania's economic, legal, and cultural reality. The Albanian Parliament has adopted a considerable number of laws and by-laws in the field of environment and, particularly, in the field of nature conservation. With all the efforts made in the legal framework, in terms of nature conservation and biological and landscape diversity, it is still difficult to ensure co-operation between institutions in implementing the law based on their legal responsibilities. The law is not uniformly practiced everywhere and provides a poor basis for the enforceability of environmental protection provisions. The stalemate in the process of drafting environmental legislation clearly reflects a low transparency and poor professionalism in all its aspects from drafting to monitoring and impact assessment.

The analysis conducted in this paper identifies problems and delays in meeting the obligations under the integration process in the field of nature conservation and biodiversity. In order to avoid these consequences, it is important for the state authorities to consider and implement at least these key measures: to accelerate and finalize the process of full harmonization of national nature conservation legislation with that of the European Union through clear transposition of European Birds and Habitats Directives; car-

---

[53]Drejt Rrjetit Natura 2000 në Shqipëri. Marrë nga adresa e internetit www.natura.al/news.php?lang=al&uid=55. Aksesuar më 08.08.2019.
[54]Ibid.

ry out the high quality and timely process of identifying potential Natura 2000 sites; until the finalization of the list of Natura 2000 sites, areas of the Emerald Network should be treated as such and managed in accordance with European Union rules and standards. Albanian state authorities should not allow projects that conflict with European Union rules and standards. If habitats or species of high conservation interest for the European Union are destroyed or damaged as a result of projects or investments permitted by the Albanian government, then this constitutes an unjustified breach of membership requirements and a direct violation of the integration process.

References

Chape, S., Spalding, M. D. & Jenkins, M. D. The World's Protected Areas: Status, Values and Prospects in the 21st Century. 376 pp. (University of California Press, 2008).

Dudley, N. (Ed.), Guidelines for Applying Protected Area Management Categories. (IUCN, 2008).

Thompson, I., B. Mackey, S. McNulty and A. Mosseler (2009); Forest Resilience, Biodiversity, and Climate Change. A synthesis of the Biodiversity/Resilience/Stability Relationship in Forest Ecosystems. Technical Series No. 43. Montreal: Secretariat of the CBD.

Ma, B.; Zhao, Z.; Ding, H.; Wen, Y. Household costs and benefits of biodiversity conservation: Case study of Sichuan giant panda reserves in China. Environ. Dev. Sustain. 2018, 20, 1665-1686.

Yang, H.; Lupi, F.; Zhang, J.; Chen, X.; Liu, J. Feedback of telecoupling: The case of a payments for ecosystem services program. Ecol. Soc. 2018, 23, 45.

Parry, M. L., O.F. Canziani, J. P. Palutikof, P. J. van der Linden and C. E. Hanson, eds. (2007); Contribution of Working Group II to the Fourth Assessment Report of the Intergovernmental Panel on Climate Change. Cambridge: Cambridge University Press.

Carroll, C., J. R. Dunk and A. Moilanen (2010); Optimizing Resiliency of Reserve Networks to Climate Change: Multispecies Conservation Planning in the Pacific Northwest, USA. Global Change Biology, 16(3): 891-904.

Ferraro, P. J.; Hanauer, M. M.; Miteva, D. A.; Nelson, J. L.; Pattanayak, S. K.; Nolte, C.; Sims, K. R. Estimating the impacts of conservation on ecosystem services and poverty by integrating modeling and evaluation. Proc. Natl. Acad. Sci. USA 2015, 112, 7420-7425.

Groves, C., M. Anderson, C. Enquist, E. Girvet, T. Sandwith, L. Schwarz and R. Shaw (2010); Climate Change and Conservation: A Primer for Assessing Impacts and Advancing Ecosystem Based Adaptation in The Nature Conservancy. Arlington, VA: TNC. 59 pp.

Palmer, M. A., D. P. Lettenmaier, N. L. Poff, S. L. Postel, B. Richter, and R. Warner (2010); Climate change and river ecosystems: protection and adaptation options. Environmental Management 44: 1053-1068.

Pour, M. D.; Motiee, N.; Barati, A. A.; Taheri, F.; Azadi, H.; Gebrehiwot, K.; Witlox, F. Impacts of the Hara biosphere reserve on livelihood and welfare in Persian Gulf. Ecol. Econ. 2017, 141, 76-86.

Hagerman, S., H. Dowlatabadi, T. Satterfield, T. McDaniels (2010); Expert views on biodiversity conservation in an era of climate change. Global Environmental Change Part A: Human & Policy Dimensions, 20(1): 192-207.

Crooks, K. R. and M. Sanjayan, eds. (2006); Connectivity Conservation. Cambridge: Cambridge University Press.

Bennett, A. F. (2003); Linkages in the Landscape: The Role of Corridors and Connectivity in Wildlife Conservation. Gland, Switzerland: IUCN.

Worboys, G. L., W. L. Francis and M. Lockwood (2010); Connectivity Conservation Management: A Global Guide. London: Earthscan.

Ben Ma, Yuqian Zhang, Yilei Hou and Yali Wen, Do Protected Areas Matter? A Systematic Review of the Social and Ecological Impacts of the Establishment of Protected Areas, International Journal of Environmental Research and Public Health, 2020, pg. 1. https://doi.org/10.3390/ijerph17197259.

Braack, L., T. Sandwith, D. Peddle, D. and T. Petermann (2006), Security Considerations in the Planning and Management of

Transboundary Conservation Areas. Gland, Switzerland: IUCN, Gland, Switzerland.

Sandwith, T., C. Shine, L. Hamilton and D. Sheppard (2001); Transboundary Protected Areas for Peace and Co-operation. Gland, Switzerland: IUCN.

UNEP-WCMC, IUCN, NGS. Protected Planet Report 2018; UNEP-WCMC, IUCN and NGS: Cambridge, UK; Gland, Switzerland; Washington, DC, USA, 2018.

FAO, UNEP. The State of the World's Forests 2020. Forests, Biodiversity and People; FAO: Rome, Italy, 2020; Available online: https://doi.org/10.4060/ca8642en (accessed on 27 September 2020).

Botim periodik i Qendrës Rajonale të Mjedisit (REC) - Shqipëri, Mjedisi Sot, Nr. 150, 2016.

Dokumenti i politikave strategjike për mbrojtjen e biodiversitetit, 2015.

Fletore Zyrtare Nr. 117.

Fletore Zyrtare nr. 7, datë 04.04.1998.

Fletore Zyrtare nr. 22, datë 2.4.2003.

Ligji Nr. 81/2017 "Për zonat e mbrojtura".

Konventa "Për tregtinë ndërkombëtare të llojeve të rrezikuara të florës dhe faunës së egër" (CITES), 22.06.1979.

Konventa e ligatinave të rëndësisë ndërkombëtare, (Ramsarit), 1971.

European Investment Bank. Environmental and Social Handbook. (2013).

European Bank for Reconstruction and Development. Environmental and Social Policy. (2014).

The World Bank. World Bank Operational Manual. Revised Version 2013. OP 4.04 Natural habitats (2013).

National Parks Directorate (2009); Principles and Guidelines for Ecological Restoration in Canada's Protected Natural Areas. Gatineau, Ontario: National Parks Directorate.

Konventa Evropiane e Peisazhit, 20.10.2000.

Konventa e Diversitetit Biologjik, ratifikuar më 05.01.1994.

EU Policy Hub, Ruajtja e natyrës dhe rëndësia e saj në procesin e integrimit, Hub Monitor, ISSUE BRIEF 30.11.2017.

Sektori i Silvikulturës, Drejtoria e Pyjeve Agjencia Kombëtare e Mjedisit, Zonat e mbrojtura, historia, gjendja dhe monitorimi, 14.04.2014.

Instituti për Ruajtjen e Natyrës në Shqipëri, Legjislacioni bazë dhe mbështetës mjedisor për menaxhimin e zonave të mbrojtura, 2017.

Komisioni Evropian, Dokument Pune i Stafit të Komisionit, Raporti i Progresit të Shqipërisë për vitin 2018, Bruksel 17.4.2018 SWD (2018) 151 final.

Komisioni Evropian, Dokument Pune i Stafit të Komisionit, Raporti i Progresit të Shqipërisë për vitin 2019, Bruksel, 29.5.2019 SWD (2019) 215 final.

www.natura.al/news.php?lang=al&uid=55.

www.ammk-rks.net/repository/docs/2_Shkurti-Dita_Nderkombetare_e_Ligatinave-Broshura.pdf.

Protected Areas for the 21st Century: Lessons from UNDP/GEF's Portofolio, pg. 17. Available: https://www.undp.org/content/dam/undp/library/Environment%20and%20Energy/biodiversity/PA_21Century.pdf.

Fit for Purpose? A Critique of the Jury System within the English and Welsh Jurisdiction

Tony Singh Purewal[1]

Abstract. Formerly taken by the members of the *assize* in its early days, the foundations of a jury predate Norman roots whereby members of the assize took the oath to justly try the cause of land disputes; although it was not until the 15th century where a jury became a part of the criminal and civil trial. Nearly 6 centuries later the general practise of jury has survived historical evolution and has become a civic duty today, however this ultimately begs the question whether a jury system is fit for purpose in a cosmopolitan and modern society despite its centrality to the English and Welsh justice system. Whilst this article does not seek to challenge the importance of the jury system, it argues that the current system is inadequate to an extent. By reflection of one's own academic and career experiences, and by exploring studies from the domains of law and psychology, this article explores whether the jury system in England and Wales is fit for purpose today in consideration of its strengths and difficulties, whilst also offering alternatives and areas for reform in response to this critique.

Keywords: Jury System, Democratic Justice, Bias, Equality, Inclusivity

[1]School of Law and Social Justice, University of Liverpool. Email: Hstpurew@liverpool.ac.uk

Introduction[2]

Whether one is a legal professional or not, the civic duty of jury service is a feature of the English and Welsh judicial system that the majority of the population are familiar with; especially when there is approximately a 40% chance of being summoned for jury service in one's lifetime.[3] However, the jury system is not a contemporary innovation to the law, but in fact a creation of the 12th century, whereby members of the *assize* took the oath to justly try the cause.[4] Trial by jury became common practise for criminal and civil trials in the 15th century, yet it only became a civic duty five centuries later. [5] Whilst there have been minor amendments to the jury system in respect of juror requirements (such as age and occupation),[6] the core foundations of deciding the culpability of the defendant(s) on the facts remains unaltered.

The jury system has persisted through years of significant historical evolution to the modern and today; this raises the question whether the jury system is fit for purpose *today*. In consideration of the advantages, difficulties, and the areas of reform for the current jury system, the main premise to the question argues that the jury system is inadequate to an extent. This article implores an in-depth analysis from three different standpoints that form a holistic and insightful analysis: as an LLB Law student, a former court official who worked under the Ministry of Justice, and most important-

---

[2]With many thanks to His Honour Judge Barrie, His Honour Judge Lowe, and the court staff at Shrewsbury Crown Court to whom guided one with a greater appreciation of the English and Welsh criminal justice system. I am grateful to their Honours and the court staff at Shrewsbury Crown Court because without such guidance, this journal article would have not been feasibly attainable.

[3]Barrett and Co Solicitors, 'Will you ever be called to Jury Service?' (*Barrett & Co*, 29th August 2018) < https://www.barrettandco.co.uk/2018/08/29/will-you-ever-be-called-to-jury-service/ > accessed 2nd August 2021.

[4]Daniel Greenberg, *Jowitts Dictionary of English Law* (5th edn, Sweet & Maxwell).

[5]Harry Kalven, 'Jury' (*Britannica*, 29th March 2019) < https://www.britannica.com/topic/jury > accessed 2nd August 2021; Juries Act 1974.

[6]Ibid n4.

ly, a former 'outsider' to Her Majesty's Courts and Tribunals Service (HMCTS). The importance behind these positions is of significance because these three standpoints enable one to approach this question with a greater appreciation of the advantages and difficulties of the jury service. Not only have these experiences enabled an in-depth analysis of the current jury system but has also assisted in offering potential alternatives and identifying areas for reform. The article builds on a substantial array of legal studies, psychological studies, and the common law throughout and contributes to the existing research literature.

A Positive Critique of the Jury System: How the System Avoids Total Inadequacy?

The jury system is the absolute pinnacle of the criminal and civil justice system in England and Wales and is therefore commendable of a positive critique that is outlined here in this first section.

Democratic-Based Justice

To truly grasp a real representation of what is meant by democratic-based justice, there are two co-existing dimensions that need to be deconstructed: democracy and the rule of law (henceforth, RoL).

The earliest existence of law predates to approximately 2100-2050 BC when the *Ur-Nammu Law Code* was created, however this idea of the RoL came later into existence by way of Athenian democracy in 500 BC.[7] Fundamentally, through an Athenian interpretation, democracy translates as the rule (*kratos*) of the people (*demos*).[8] For the Athenians, democracy was pivotal in emancipating and providing further power to the *demos* (people), and consequently, this is where the law became a core ele-

[7]Samuel Noah Kramer, 'Ur-Nammu Law Code' [1954] GBP Vol. 23(1), 40-51; Mogens Herman Hansen, *Brill's Companion to the Reception of Athenian Democracy* (Brill 2020) 27-54.

[8]Mogens (n6).

ment of democracy.[9] This becomes particularly important for conceptions regarding the RoL, because by incorporating law and democracy together, it had enabled the Athenians to recodify and republish bodies of law.[10] Academics, such as Forsdyke, have suggested that the Athenians provided a foundation for the modern conventions of the RoL by recognising three substantial elements: legal supremacy, legal equality, and legal certainty.[11]

However, there is a general consensus among academics that the RoL was first established later in 350 BC (approximate), by Aristotle.[12] In approaching his theory to the RoL, Aristotle contended that the law was advantageous in terms of governance: '*laws are made after long consideration, whereas decisions in the court are given at short notice, which makes it hard for those to try the case to satisfy the claims of justice'*.[13] Aristotle's theory suggested that bodies of law could not be applied broadly, which resonates with his further works that mention the RoL.[14]For instance, in *Politics* Aristotle questioned whether the law is to be ruled by man or the best law.[15] Throughout time there has been significant development concerning the RoL; however, the most notable and 'contemporary' understanding is reflected in Dicey's 'exposition' of the RoL.[16] Dicey has developed three principles whereby legal matters of man are to be conducted in the correct legal manner, the law should apply equally to all, and society should 'conform' to the RoL.[17]

---

[9]Daniela Louise Cammack, 'Rethinking Athenian Democracy' (Doctoral Dissertation, Harvard University 2013), 6.

[10]Cammack (n8).

[11]Sara Forsdyke, 'Ancient and Modern Conceptions of the Rule of Law' [2019] University Press Scholarship Online

[12]Jeremy Waldron, 'Is the Rule of Law an Essentially Contested Concept (in Florida)?' [2002] 21 Law & Philosophy 137, 141.

[13]Aristotle, *Art of Rhetoric* (≈350 BC), 1354b.

[14]Jeremy Waldron, 'The Rule of Law' (*Stanford Encyclopaedia of Philosophy*, 22 June 2016) < https://plato.stanford.edu/entries/rule-of-law/#Aris > accessed 9 August 2021.

[15]Aristotle, *Politics* (≈350 BC), 1282b.

[16]Albert Venn Dicey, *Introduction to the Study of the Law of the Constitution* (1885).

[17]Constitution Committee, *Paper by Professor Paul Craig: The Rule of Law* (HL 2006-07)

Whilst it can be assumed that democracy emancipates the power of the people and that the RoL is important for equality and fairness, interdependence can be established between the RoL and democracy.[18] This link is of prominence within the criminal and civil justice system and can therefore be sought to provide a logical reasoning for the features of a modern jury system. For instance, Aristotle's theory outlined in *Rhetoric* demonstrates that general bodies of law cannot be applied equally because each case is unique. Not only has the RoL played a central role in widening the gap of access to justice, but Aristotle's theory is also reflected in the careful procedures that a jury should take in trying the case "*to satisfy the claims of justice*".[19] In a similar manner, Dicey's notion of social equality before the law is reminiscent of the 'power of the people' concept that has been defined under Athenian democracy. Such ideas of democracy suggest that there should be a requirement that the *demos* (people) have their say within legal matters, especially in relation to criminal and civil matters that may directly affect the general public. In consideration of these ideas surrounding democratic justice, one could argue that it would, in fact, be undemocratic to prohibit the *demos* (people) from trying defendants in criminal and civil trials because it is their democratic right to do so. In any sense, the *demos* (people) cannot be lawmakers as it reserves these positions for those in the highest offices, but a trial by jury provides an approach that strikes the balance between the democratic and legal functions of society by enabling the people to determine the culpability of those criminally indicted.

A Standardised Procedure

Standardisation refers to the 'replicability' of procedures and is thus regarded as an '*efficient technique for facilitating both internal consistency and replication*'.[20] Although considered a scientific procedure, it can be said that the jury procedure is also a stan-

---

[18]Rule of Law Alliance, 'Impact of Rule of Law: Rule of Law & Democracy' (*Rule of Law Alliance*, 2016) < rolalliance.org/rol-alliance-impact/rule-of-law-democracy/> accessed 10 August 2021.

[19]Aristotle (n14).

[20]Darwin Weinberg 'standardization' in George Ritzer, *The Blackwell Encyclopedia of Sociology* (Blackwell Publishing 2006).

dardised procedure. Given that trials by jury predate to 1215, it would be feasibly impossible to provide an accurate figure for the amount of jury trials that have occurred over the years.[21] Alternatively, an appreciation to the amount of conducted jury trials can be found in the Ministry of Justice's statistics quarterly.[22] As a result of the detriment posed by the COVID-19 on jury trials, statistics from 2019 demonstrate a better insight; the data reveal that around 100,000 criminal cases were disposed of in the Crown court, of which 38% (38,000) were trials for triable-either-way offences, and 22% (22,000) were for indictable offences.[23] These figures will not be concurrent with the number of trials taken prior to 2019, but they provide an overall insight into the level of standardisation that takes place. Conventionally, the Crown Court has adopted a set of standardised and replicated procedures across England and Wales.

In addition to the jury procedures, standardisation is also prevalent in ensuring fair trials. Such examples can be identified in the judge's strict warning to the jury about disclosure of the deliberations, and this has even been extended to include codification in legislation.[24] Within the context of the court, there have been instances where a juror has been discharged for possessing a 'guilty' predisposition against the defendant before the evidence has been presented.[25] All of these instances are stand

[21]Geoffrey Robertson, 'Magna Carta and jury trial' [2015] British Library.

[22]Ministry of Justice, 'Criminal justice statistics quarterly' (*GOV UK*, 22 August 2013) <www.gov.uk/government/collections/criminal-justice-statistics-quarterly> accessed 12 August 2021.

[23]Georgina Sturge, Court statistics for England and Wales (House of Commons Library Briefing Paper CBP 8372, 2020) <www.researchbriefings.files.parliament.uk/documents/CBP-8372/CBP-8372.pdf> accessed 22 December 2020

[24]Juries Act 1974.

[25] Based on the author's personal experience.

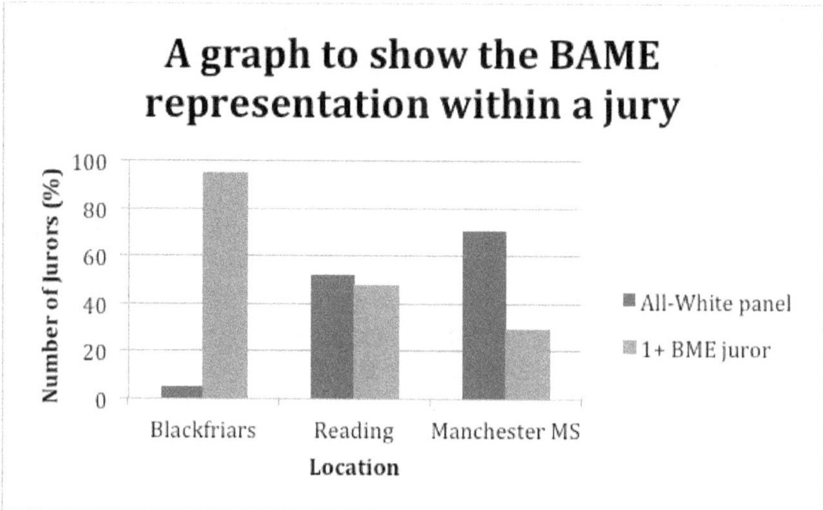

ardised examples of protecting the right to a fair trial.[26] On the grounds of both points regarding standardisation, face validity (a test of internal validity) can be satisfied because the procedures of standardisation have been successful in bestowing a verdict or 'delivering justice'.[27] However, this raises a predicament because validity and reliability are often regarded interchangeably. Just because validity can be established, this does not necessarily mean the jury system is a reliable approach.[28] Nevertheless, the practise of standardisation undeniably takes place within the jury system.

Collectivist Rather Than Individualistic

As opposed to individualism, where one is motivated by an independent social pattern concerned with individualistic preferences, collectivism is where the goals of the collective are prioritised over the individual.[29] In the United Kingdom, a study by Geert Hofstede

[26]Convention for the Protection of Human Rights and Fundamental Freedoms (European Convention on Human Rights, as amended) (ECHR) article 6.

[27]John Gaber 'face validity' in Neil Joseph Salkind, *Encylopedia of Research Design* (SAGE Publications 2010).

[28]Pamela Moss, 'Can There Be Validity without Reliability?' [1994] AERA 23(2), 5-12.

[29]Harry Triandis, *Individualism & collectivism* (1st edn, Routledge 1995), 2.

revealed that the UK scores highly amongst other countries with an individualistic score of 89.[30] In spite of this, the jury system revolves around the vitality of the collective. This is demonstrated within the composition of 12 jurors that have to reach a unanimous verdict, which ultimately derives from its history where land disputes would be resolved collectively by a unanimous vote of 12 witnesses.[31] The importance of a unanimous vote is still prevalent today, and judges often direct the jury to 'strive' for a unanimous decision; on the contrary, if all the jurors cannot reach a unanimous verdict, a majority verdict will be accepted.[32]

The advantageous position of the collective is that it gives rise to an '*exposure (of)... new ideas, methodologies, and insights*', whereas for individualism, the sole responsibility is an area of difficulty.[33] Furthermore, it would require one to possess an expansive skill set in approaching conceptual, methodological and technical issues simultaneously.[34] The collective approach is therefore particularly favoured within jury deliberations because it is less common that 12 people will forget the minute details (in comparison to an individual) and ensures these meticulous details are considered such that a unanimous decision can be sought.[35] In addition, the idea of a unanimous decision is important because it reflects. and links to, the idea of democratic-based justice; in fact, a study revealed that the initial position favoured by jurors at the start of

---

[30]Hofstede Insights, 'What about the UK?' (*Hofstede Insights*, n.d.) <www.hofstede-insights.com/country/the-uk/ > accessed 13 August 2021.

[31]Tana Adkin QC, 'Guest blog: How will restricting jury trial and reducing jury numbers affect the delivery of justice?' (*The Bar Council*, 10 July 2020) <www.barcouncil.org.uk/resource/guest-blog-how-will-restricting-jury-trial-and-reducing-jury-numbers-affect-the-delivery-of-justice.html> accessed 13 August 2021.

[32]Criminal Practise Directions (2015), VI Trial 26(1).

[33]Andrew Kemp, 'Collaboration v Individualism: What Is Better for the Rising Academic?' [2013] TQR 18(50), 4-6.

[34]Kemp [n31].

[35]William Hirst, Alin Coman and Charles Stone, 'Memory and Jury Deliberation: The Benefits and Costs of Collective Remembering' in Lynn Nadel and Walter Sinnot Armstrong, *Memory and Law* (Oxford Scholarship Online 2012).

the trial becomes the verdict in around 90% of cases.[36] While this could indicate the advantageous position of unanimous verdicts, it also raises doubts because, as one study suggests, jury members are not "*willing to change their minds*" –that is, the initial impressions of jury members tend to remain the same irrespective of the evidence presented in the court room.[37] For these reasons, the collective nature of the jury system prevails, because an individualistic approach could be inappropriate. This point will be analysed further in the next section.

Equality and Inclusivity

Equality and inclusivity are ubiquitous terms that are at the heart of every notable institution and, on the surface, have been applied within the jury system where everybody's judgement matters.

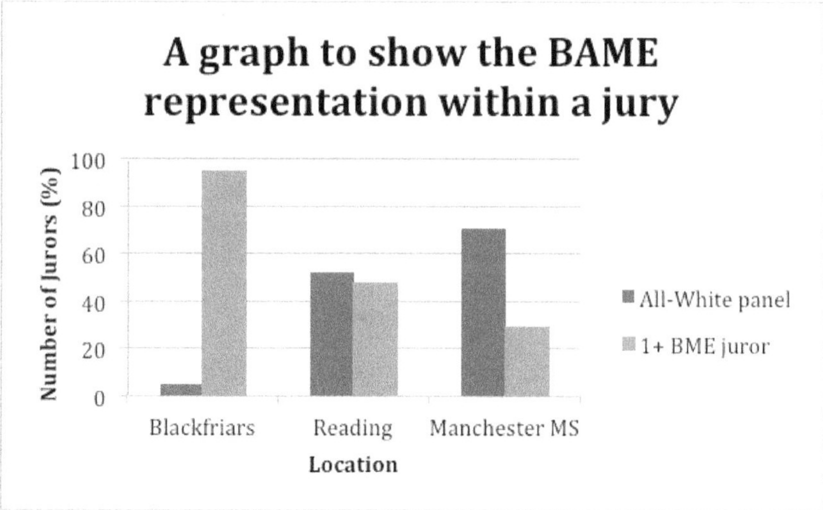

Figure 1.4.1: BAME Representation in Blackfriars, Reading and Manchester (Thomas, 2007)

[36]Brian Bornstein and Edie Greene, 'Jury Decision Making: Implications for and From Psychology' [2011] SAGE 20(1), 65.

[37]Daphna Oyserman and Ayse Uskul, 'Individualism and collectivism: Societal-level processes with implications for individual-level and society-level outcomes' in Fons van de Vijer, Dianne van Hemert and Ype Poortinga, *Multilevel Analysis of Individuals and Cultures* (Taylor & Francis 2008).

The participation of ethnicity and religion remains an ambiguous element of the jury system because, considering Cheryl Thomas's study, disparity can be established amongst BAME participation across three varying locations: Blackfriars, Reading and Manchester.[38] It should be highlighted how Thomas's study was conducted in 2007 and therefore serves as the closest study, at least officially, that discusses diversity and fairness within the jury system today. Figure 1 presents the disparity from where there is at least more than one BAME juror in Blackfriars, as opposed to the disparities in Reading and Manchester MS.[39] Undeniably, there is BAME representation, but an ambiguous element arises from such lack of geographical consistency.

Socioeconomic

Socioeconomic status can be measured by considering the factor of one's occupation. Despite certain professions being exempt from jury service (such as those who work in the criminal justice system),[40] Thomas found that "*no occupational groups were significantly under-represented among serving jurors*".[41] As a result, this means that a doctor or an accountant. for instance, has an equal position with a cleaner in reaching a fair decision and can thus ensure that a verdict reflects an all-rounded judgement.

Gender

Prior to 1921, women were banned from sitting on a jury; with some progression, women cannot be discriminated against for sitting on a jury.[42] Fortunately, the position today indicates that there is representation of both males and females in any case; Thomas found that 88% of juries had either a 6:6, 7:5 or 8:4 gender split,

---

[38]Cheryl Thomas and Nigel Balmer, *Diversity and Fairness in the Jury System* (Ministry of Justice Research No.2, 2007).

[39]Thomas (n36) 147.

[40]HM Courts & Tribunal Service, 'Guide to jury summons' (*GOV UK*, 1 July 2017) <www.gov.uk/government/publications/guide-to-jury-summons> accessed 17 August 2021.

[41]Thomas (n36) 137.

[42]Sex Disqualification (Removal) Act 1919.

and can be commended in ensuring gender equality within the jury.[43]

Age

One requirement of the jury service is that a juror should be aged between 18 and 76 years old, which enables the young and old to participate in delivering justice.[44] While most ages can take part within a jury, Thomas found that across all three courts majority of the jurors are aged between 30-44, although this does vary geographically. [45] This is reflected in one's own experiences of dealing with older jurors, because within Shropshire there is a higher percentage of over 65's in comparison to the national average.[46] Regardless of this fact, the jury system embraces both young and old within the jury system.

Disabilities

Currently, there are no formal statistics that can provide an overview for the number of disabled jurors that can be accounted for; though, this does not mean jurors with disabilities are excluded. In fact, jurors with disabilities have reasonable adjustments that are disabled-friendly in order to satisfy the jurors' requirements. Examples of reasonable adjustments include accessible amenities around the courts (lifts, ramps etc), hearing loops and even the benefit of a sign language interpreter.[47] All of these adjustments have made the jury system open and more equal for disabled jurors.

Overall, on the surface, the jury system is both equal and inclusive for all jurors.

---

[43]Thomas (n36) 144.

[44]Juries Act 1974, Section 1(1)(a).

[45]Thomas (n36) 142.

[46]Shropshire Council, Population (*Shropshire Council*, 2011) <www.shropshire.gov.uk/information-intelligence-and-insight/facts-and-figures/population/> accessed 17 August 2021.

[47]Ministry of Justice. 'Law change opens door to deaf jurors' (*GOV UK*, 9 March 2021) <www.gov.uk/government/news/law-change-opens-door-to-deaf-jurors> accessed 17 August 2021.

A Negative Critique of the Jury System: How and Where the Jury System Becomes Partially Inadequate?

On the other hand, there are issues within the jury system that indicate its inadequacy in some areas; this section therefore analyses and explores the negative criticism of the jury system.

Representation in Focus

As noted in Section 1, BAME represent a portion of the jury but there is a lack of geographical consistency between a panel of jurors, with more than one BAME juror and an all-white jury panel. Building on this, the following paragraphs analyse how this lack of geographical consistency has impacted jury proceedings and their verdicts.

Consistent representation is important because of its effect in jury deliberations. Valerie Hans noted that "*the inclusion of minorities and women in the representative jury adds their life experiences and insights to the collective pool of knowledge*",[48] which is reflected in differing conviction rates. For instance, an American study revealed that there are higher conviction rates for white defendants and lower conviction rates for black defendants when there is more than one black juror.[49] These findings could indicate how verdicts can vary because of representation. Nevertheless, the current jury system relies on the electoral register, such that the judge or counsel cannot select a juror based on personal characteristics.[50]

---

[48]Neil Vidmar and Valerie Hans, *American Juries: The Verdict* (Prometheus Books, 2007), 74.

[49]Shamena Anwar, Patrick Bayer and Randi Hjalmarsson, 'The Impact of Jury Race in Criminal Trials' [2012] The Quarterly Journal of Economics 127(2), 1019.

[50]GOV UK, 'Jury Service' (*GOV UK*, N/D) < https://www.gov.uk/jury-service > accessed 19 August 2021.

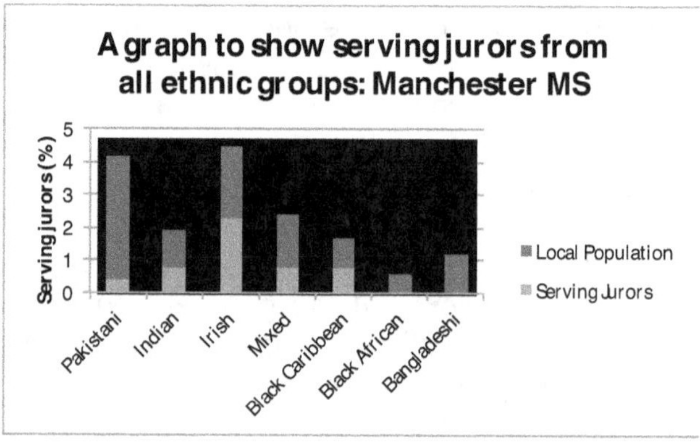

Figure 2.1.1: variability among juror ethnicity (Thomas, 2007)

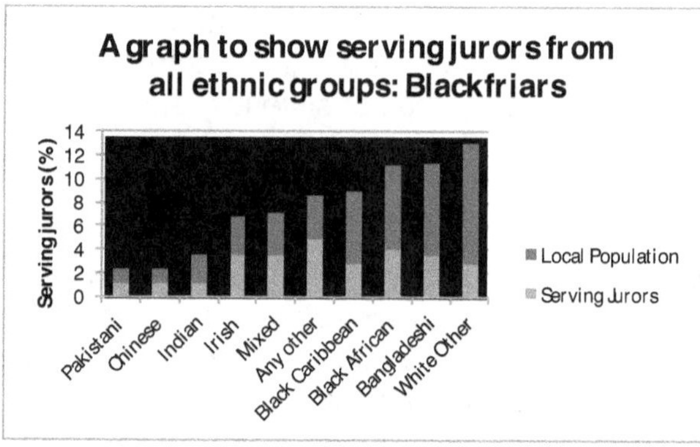

Figure 2.1.2: a comparison of jurors' ethnic groups (Thomas, 2007)

As the electoral register operates based on randomisation, it is presumably unbiased and fair; yet, this has had consequences because it has not ensured proportional or equal representation. The term BAME stands for Black, Asian and minority ethnic.[51] It is a loose term that fails to account for the breakdown of differing ethnic groups, and Thomas displays this breakdown quantitatively. Equal and proportional representation is of importance because, in consideration of Hans' statement in the previous paragraph, there is a great variability among different ethnic groups.[52] In other

[51]Peter J. Aspinall, 'BAME (black, Asian and minority ethnic): the 'new normal' in collective terminology' [2021] Journal of Epidemiology & Community Health.75(2), 107.

[52]Hans (n46).

words, the experiences of one ethnic group cannot be standardised for those of other ethnic groups. This is demonstrated by Figure 2 and Figure 3, which show not only a lack of consistency, but also a limited proportionality between ethnic groups (with the exception of Irish and White-British).[53]

Geographical differences can be acknowledged, for example, Pakistanis in Blackfriars are proportionally represented as opposed to Manchester MS; but the general trends show there is disproportionality among ethnic groups, such as Black African and Bangladeshi ethnic groups, for instance. Thomas suggests that it is a 'myth' that BAME groups are underrepresented yet the disproportionality, as evidenced above, suggests that some ethnic groups have been underrepresented at the expense of other ethnic groups being over-represented.[54] Although, despite the blatant barriers of the electoral register in jury summoning, there is room for improvement in achieving consistency and proportionality.

Unconscious Bias

Unconscious bias (UB) refers to the mental associations held by a social group that shares certain characteristics and produces negative evaluations and stereotypes.[55] UB can be viewed as an umbrella term that encompasses biases against gender, sex, socioeconomic status, and race, among other factors that produce inequalities in modern society. Research has particularly found how 'statistically significant unwarranted racial disparity exists', which impacts the confidence of the public in the criminal justice system.[56]

---

[53]Thomas (n36) 128-130.

[54]Thomas (n36) 192.

[55]Chloe FitzGerald and others, 'Interventions designed to reduce implicit prejudices and implicit stereotypes in real world contexts: a systematic review' [2019] BMC Psychology 7(29), 1.

[56]Ojmarrh Mitchell, 'A Meta-Analysis of Race and Sentencing Research: Explaining the Inconsistencies' [2005] JQC 21(4), 463; RP Advisors, *Reducing Racial Disparity in the Criminal Justice System: A Manual for Practitioners and Policymakers* (The Sentencing Project, 2008) 62.

Race

Particularly within recent years, racial UB in jury deliberations has been subjected to criticism internationally.[57] UB has come to light in the American study conducted by Sunnafrank and Fontes, because of findings that white jurors often associate 'white-collar' (fraud) crimes with white defendants in comparison to the association of violent crimes with black defendants.[58] These examples of UB have a detrimental influence on conviction rates, as it has been reported that young males with parents of different ethnicities are 2.7 times more likely of being prosecuted compared to young males with white parents.[59] Irrespective of these statistics, one should remember the extent to which racial biases had played in the case of *R v Mirza,* where jury impropriety resulted from the defendants' race.[60] However, this is not the only documented case of racially biased jury impropriety, but this was similarly observed in the deliberations of *R v Qureshi.*[61] Both these cases are prominent examples of racial bias in jury deliberations, which questions the extent to which racial UB in jury deliberations has occurred, but has not been documented. Nevertheless, courts have demonstrated that when judges take appropriate steps in their directions when dealing with claims of racism within a jury, as in the case of *Gregory* and *Smith*, race becomes irrelevant.[62] Although, considering *Gregory* in light of Sunnafrank and Fontes' research, racial bias can still take place through the UB of a juror regardless of whether a judge has dealt with the factor of racial bias in their directions or not; the point is that a juror would not

[57]Gillian Daly and Rosemary Pattenden, 'Racial Bias and the English Criminal Trial Jury' [2005] The Cambridge Law Journal 64(3); Jennifer Elek and Paula Hannaford-Agor, 'First, Do No Harm: On Addressing the Problem of Implicit Bias in Juror Decision Making' [2013] The Journal of the American Judges Association 404.

[58]Michael Sunnafrank and Norman Fontes, 'General and Crime Relates Racial Stereotypes and Influence on Juridic Decisions' [1983] Cornell Journal of Social Relations 17(1).

[59]Tiggey May and others, 'Differential treatment in the youth justice system' [2010] Equality and Human Rights Commission Research report 50.

[60]*R v Mirza* [2004] Crim 1235.

[61]*R v Qureshi* [2001] EWCA Crim 1807.

[62]*R v Smith* [2003] EWCA Crim 283; *Gregory v UK* [1997] ECHR 25.

know whether they are being racially biased or not because it is unconscious. [63] For these reasons, UB becomes an area that needs to be addressed and improved due to its blatant limitations on a fair trial.

Other Factors: Gender and Socioeconomic

As previously mentioned, UB also concerns gender and one's socioeconomic. In terms of gender, research has shown that UB occurs in rape trials where there is lack of physical injury and emotional response on behalf of the victim, which could lead to a 'not guilty' verdict.[64] The reality, however, is that physical injury and a specific emotional response is not necessarily required in rape cases because each case differs.[65] In a similar manner to race and gender, UB can also have a detrimental role in the c of one's socioeconomic background. This remains an area of contention as some academics argue that the defendant's social background is largely unimportant in guilty verdicts, yet simultaneously, some academics have argued that one's socioeconomic does exert influence in jury trials.[66] Emmelman established that socioeconomic biases arise by way of '*class-linked behaviour tendencies'* and hence argues that '*its influence (socioeconomic bias) is considerably greater than any of us have realised'*.[67] Notwithstanding the contention of UB in a socioeconomic context, it would not be unreasonable to suggest that UB occurs within a socioeconomic context in addition to the defendant's gender and race.

---

[63]Ibid (n24).

[64]Louise Ellison and Vanessa Munro, 'Reacting to Rape: Exploring Mock Jurors' Assessments of Complaints Credibility' [2009] The British Journal of Criminology 49(2), 202-219.

[65]Ellison and Munro (n60); Ellen Wessel, 'Credibility of the emotional witness: a study of ratings by court judges' [2006] Law and Human Behaviour 30, 221-230.

[66]Robert Gordon and Paul Jacobs, 'Forensic Psychology: Perception of Guilt and Income' [1969] Perceptual and Motor Skills 28(1), 143-146; Debra Emmelman, 'The Effect of Social Class on the Adjudication of Criminal Cases: Class-linked Behaviour Tendencies Common Sense and the Interpretive Procedures of Court-appointed Defence Attorneys' [1994] Symbolic Interaction 17(1), 1-20.

[67]Emmelman (n62), 14-16.

Conformity

The basic definition of conformity refers to the 'act of fitting in with the group', but this is a form of social influence that can arise in three forms: compliance (the individual adopts the induced behaviour regardless of their own beliefs), identification (the individual conforms to their social role), and internalisation (the individual adopts the induced behaviour).[68] For the purposes of this article, compliance and identification are relevant because they are prevalent in the explanation for conformity discussed in this article: normative social influence (a term for where one conforms to fit in with the social group).[69] Throughout these paragraphs, these terms will assist in demonstrating the extent to which conformity and social influence has on decision-making processes that are utilised during jury deliberations.

Solomon Asch's ground-breaking psychological study on conformity has demonstrated the extent to which an individual conforms in the presence of a majority.[70] Asch found that around 75% of participants conformed at least once in over 12 clinical trials, and thus concluded that this was either because of normative social influence or because they believe the social group has better knowledge than themselves (known as informational social influence).[71] In later studies though, Asch did find that there were situational variables that included group size, task difficulty and even

---

[68]Julie Coultas and Edwin van Leeuwen, 'Conformity: Definitions, Types and Evolutionary Grounding' in Virgil Zeigler-Hill, Lisa Welling and Todd Shackelford, *Evolutionary Perspectives on Social Psychology* (Springer, 2015), 189; Herbert Kelman, 'Compliance, identification and internalization: three processes of attitude change' [1958] The Journal of Conflict Resolution 2(1), 53.

[69]Robert Burnkrant and Alan Cousineau, 'Informational and Normative Social Influence in Buyer Behaviour' [1975] Journal of Consumer Research 2(3), 207.

[70]Solomon Asch, 'Effects of group pressure upon the modification and distortion of judgement' in Harold Guetzkow, *Groups, leadership and men; research in human relations* (Carnegie Press, 1951).

[71]Asch (n66).

a variation where participants could answer in private.[72] These studies suggested that conformity increased with a larger group and with a more difficult test, yet conversely found conformity decreased when the participant answered in private.

Some academics have criticised Asch's study as having low ecological validity in suggesting that it does not reflect real life scenarios; however, Penrod and Hastie found that there is a '*momentum effect'* within juries where members of the minority begin to join the majority.[73] Consequently, this questions the overall validity of jury verdicts and echoes Miller and Bornstein's opinion that a "*defendant is entitled to a verdict that reflect the jurors' genuine beliefs, not one made to conform to normative pressures*".[74] All things considered, it is unclear whether such verdicts are a product of genuine normative social influence or by the very fact that a jury is encouraged to reach a unanimous verdict. Furthermore, this is complicated by contrasting studies that argue there is no determinable link between conformity and their verdicts produced in jury deliberations.[75] It is, in this instance, an ambiguous yet perceptive critique of the jury system.

The Reasonable Person Standard

The term 'reasonable person' is associated with criminal and negligence law to demonstrate that the defendant's actions were simi-

[72]Solomon Asch, 'Group forces in the modification and distortion of judgements' in Solomon Asch, *Social Psychology* (Oxford University Press, 1952), 450-501; Solomon Asch, 'Studies of independence and conformity: I. A minority of one against a unanimous majority' [1956] Psychological Monographs: General and applied 70(9), 1-70.

[73]Saul Mcleod, 'Solomon Asch – Conformity Experiment' (*Simply Psychology*, 28 December 2018) < https://www.simplypsychology.org/asch-conformity.html > accessed 25 August 2021; Steven Penrod and Reid Hastie, 'A computer simulation of jury decision making' [1980] Psychological Review 87(2), 133-159.

[74]Monica Miller and Brian Bornstein, 'Do juror pressures lead to unfair verdicts' [2008] Monitor of Psychology 39(3), 18.

[75]Ashley Bowser, 'To Conform or Not to Conform: An Examination of the Effects of Mock Jury Deliberation on Individual Jurors' (Electronic Theses and Dissertations, Tennessee State University 2013) 1164.

lar to that of the average person.[76] Though the standard is being used as an analogy for addressing the pitfalls when jurors fail to satisfy this standard. One would argue, here, that this standard fails due to a genuine lack of knowledge or ignorance.

Genuine Lack of Knowledge

A genuine lack of knowledge refers to the jurors' ability to comprehend the evidence and legal directions. A Scottish study revealed that, in a mock jury, 14 out of 64 juries contradicted the judge's directions regarding the burden and standard of proof ('*presumed innocent unless found guilty*').[77] In response to similar concerns, Koehler has suggested that jurors should be trained through empirically based and standardised training modules in teaching jurors how to make effective decisions and avoid common misconception that result in unfair verdicts.[78] Although, certainly within England and Wales, jurors are consistently reminded that they are judges of fact and not the law; so, accuracy is dependent on the jurors' engagement throughout the trial.

Ignorance

Ignorance is seemingly a conspicuous point, but it is nevertheless, credible. The term 'stealth juror', where a juror conceals their bias (from the judge and barristers) in their aim to influence the trial, becomes relevant here.[79] Stealth jurors are perilous to the jury

[76]Macmillan Dictionary, 'the reasonable person' (*Macmillan dictionary*, N/D) <www.macmillandictionary.com/dictionary/british/the-reasonable-person#:~:text=UK%EE%A8%A6%20%2F%CB%8Cri%CB%90z(%C9%99),Synonyms%20and%20related%20word> accessed 26 August 2021.

[77]Rachel Ormston and others, 'Scottish Jury Research: Findings from a Large-Scale Mock Jury Study' [2019] Social Research Series (10/19).

[78]Jonathan Koehler, 'Train Our Jurors' (Faculty Working Papers, Northwestern University School of Law 2006) Paper 141, 322-323.

[79]American Psychological Association, 'APA Dictionary of Psychology: stealth juror' (*American Psychological Association*, N/D) <www.dictionary.apa.org/stealth-juror> accessed 26 August 2021.

proceedings because they could deny that they do not know the defendant or witness during the empanelling process, but they could also allow their own personal views to influence the verdict instead of the legal facts during deliberations.[80] This has been known to occur in many cases, including the murder trial of Scott Peterson whereby three jurors allegedly lied to serve on the trial.[81] Whilst the defence counsel argued this was for monetary benefit, it nevertheless highlights conscious ignorance.[82]

Both of these failures cannot be ignored because it should be remembered that this is a matter of justice and one's life, so these failures limit access to justice.

A Multitude of Logistical Errors

In assessing the logistical errors of the jury system, there are two particular focal points: efficiency and expenses.

Efficiency

The first point regarding efficiency concerns the times and delays that are resultant of jury trials. On average, trial hearings take 15.3 hours (not guilty).[83] For deliberations this can differ, but the general rule is that two hours should at least pass before a majority direction can be given.[84] It should be noted that these statistics do not include delays and are representative of the timings prior to COVID-19, which raises particular concern in lieu with the backlog

---

[80]Dena DaSilva, 'The Stealth Juror' (*Jury Analyst*, 15 August 2015) <www.juryanalyst.com/blog/the-stealth-juror/> accessed 26 August 2021.

[81] *The People of the State of California v Scot Lee Peterson* [2004] SC 55500.

[82]Stacy Finz, 'Peterson Prosecutors call any move to L.A. a bad trip' (*San Francisco Chronicle Archive* in *SFGATE*, May 11 2004) <www.sfgate.com/bayarea/article/REDWOOD-CITY-Peterson-prosecutors-call-any-move-2780548.php> accessed 26 August 2021.

[83]Ministry of Justice, 'Criminal court statistics quarterly, England and Wales' (*GOV UK*, 29 September 2016) <www.assets.publishing.service.gov.uk/government/uploads/system/uploads/attachment_data/file/556442/ccsq-bulletin.pdf> accessed 27 August 2021.

[84]Juries Act 1974, section 17(4).

of cases the courts face. As it stands today, there is substantial concern over the backlog of cases as they have rose by 17,000 within the Crown court.[85] On the other hand, achieving justice requires an extensive amount of time.[86] While this would be a reasonable contention, it should be remembered that this backlog is only growing significantly.

Expenses

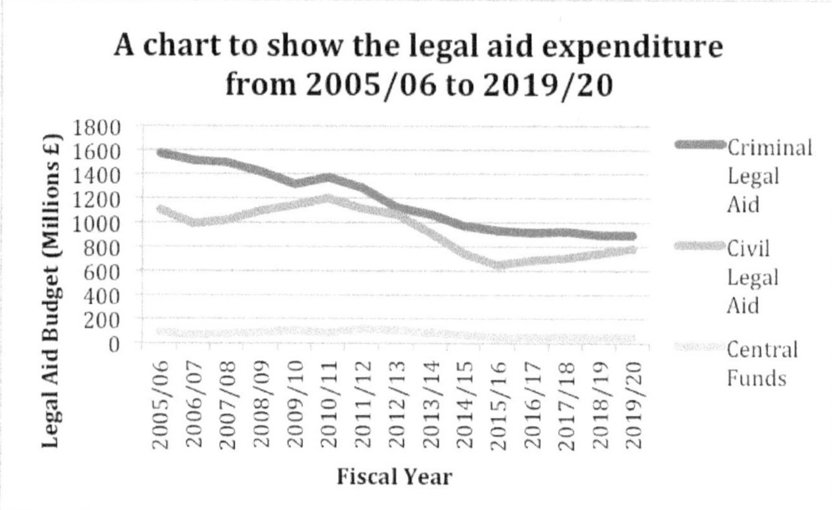

Figure 2.5.2.1

The average ten-day serving juror amounts to approximately £70.66 per day (not inclusive of travel). [87] An accurately calculated figure for annual juror expenses cannot be calculated, but it can be suggested that juror expenses are highly priced. When considering the striking cuts that have been made to the legal aid budget in the legal aid crisis (figure 4), it is questionable whether cuts could be made to the juror expenses budget and redirected to the

[85]Select Committee on the Constitution, *COVID-19 and the Courts* (HL 2019-20, 257), para 131.

[86]Aristocles (Plato), *The Republic* (≈375BC) 443c-e.

[87]GOV UK, 'Jury Service: What you can claim if you're an employee' (*GOV UK*, N/D) < https://www.gov.uk/jury-service/what-you-can-claim-if-youre-an-employee > accessed 27 August 2021.

legal aid budget.[88] Although it is difficult for the judiciary to establish where the priorities lie, here it is argued that it would be unreasonable to redirect and make cuts to the juror expense budget because it is ultimately a separate issue. In any event, however, access to justice remains restricted because the opposite will just prevail.

Uncontrolled Factors

Notably, there are further factors that are inconsistent with, and uncontrolled by, the court. These include situations within the Crown Court, such as when the prosecution counsel did not read the name of a witness during empanelling, which led to the juror later being discharged because they had recognised that witness. Furthermore, there have been occasions when a serving juror believed they did not need to be present despite being told beforehand. These situations cannot be controlled yet provide significant obstacles in the course of a jury trial.

Moving Forwards with the Current Jury System

Reforming the Current System

The first subsection discusses potential areas for reform in response to the issues that were highlighted in the negative critique of the jury system.

Representation

Research has demonstrated how BAME representation amongst jurors is not geographically consistent, nor is it often proportional

[88]Sarah Moore and Alex Newbury, *Legal aid in crisis: Assessing the impact of reform* (Bristol University Press, 2017); D. Clark, 'Legal Aid Spending in England and Wales 2005-2020' (*Statista*, 2 November 2020) < https://www.statista.com/statistics/1098628/legal-aid-spending-in-england-and-wales/#statisticContainer > accessed 27 August 2021.

with local populations.[89] In response to similar issues, lessons could be learnt from other judicial jurisdictions. For instance, the United States attempted to tackle racial representation in American juries by diverting attention to voter registration (used in jury summoning) to include more ethnic minorities.[90] Aside from this initiative, it has been suggested that one way to improve diversity in jury summons is to implement a diversity quota that ensures there is a minimum of one BAME representative among jurors.[91] Although, this would be administratively unfeasible because jury summons are randomised. Ironically, the effect of randomisation can be seen where resident judge, His Honour Judge Keith Cutler, received a jury summon to serve as a juror at his own court in Salisbury.[92] A problem that may arise from implementing a diversity quota (a minimum of BAME jury member) is that such selective process inevitably provides the grounds for potential prospective bias because, as explained by Alschuler, this could encourage juror's to perceive themselves/others in racial terms that could give likely to the persistence of 'racially distinctive viewpoints'.[93]

Unconscious Bias

UB can affect the proceedings of jury trials and, as revealed by statistics, could be dangerous to jurors' verdicts.[94] To address this issue, UB training may provide a solution against the effects of racial bias on decision making in court.[95] On the one hand, UB training requires minimum effort and is cost-effective, taking ad-

[89]Thomas (n36).

[90]Thomas (n36) 10.

[91]Hiroshi Fukurai, 'A Quota Jury: Affirmative Action in Jury Selection' [1997] Journal of Criminal Justice 25(6).

[92]Ben Mitchell, 'Judge excused from jury service because he was presiding over case' (*The Independent*, 16 April 2020) <www.independent.co.uk/news/uk/home-news/judge-jury-service-court-trial-salisbury-winchester-keith-cutler-a8872611.html> accessed 9 December 2021

[93]Albert Alschuler, 'Racial Quotas and the Jury' [1996] DLJ 44(4), 34.

[94]May (n55).

[95]Elek (n53).

vantage of online training, designed by specialists. [96] On the other hand, academics have suggested that UB training is only effective when a prospective juror can actually apply the lessons to their service and consciously engage with training. [97] As previously stated, whilst there is a gap in research that does support the efficacy of UB training in a court environment, it can be said that the efficacy of UB training is largely reliant on the engagement of the jury.

Conformity

Conformity in jury trials is an ambiguous area, but certainly one that should not be disregarded. In a similar approach to UB, academics have suggested the implementation of training for group decision-making to improve group dynamics.[98] This, however, raises concerns about the effectiveness of training because, in most cases, conformity (as detailed earlier) can occur unconsciously. Furthermore, it raises doubts in relation to the 'unanimous verdict' criteria outlined in the judge's directions because it could arguably reinforce conformity.[99] Whilst it can be appreciated that the judge can accept a majority verdict, this does not necessarily mean conformity can arise in reaching a unanimous verdict, since a juror could conform with other jurors in order to reach a unanimous verdict. In respect of these concerns, it is suggested that a majority verdict is a suitable position for reducing conformity in jury trials.

---

[96] Equality and Diversity UK, 'Unconscious Bias Training Course' (*Equality and Diversity UK*, N/D) <www.equalityanddiversity.co.uk/unconscious-bias-training-course.htm> accessed 31 August 2021.

[97] Anona Su, 'A Proposal to Properly Address Implicit Bias in the Jury' [2020] Hastings Women's Law Journal 31(1) 6.

[98] Sara Gordon, 'All Together Now: Using Principles of Group Dynamics to Train Better Jurors' (Scholarly Commons, UNLV Williams S. Boyd School of Law 2015) 896.

[99] Jason Reichelt, 'Standing Alone: Conformity, Coercion, and the Protection of the Holdout Juror' [2007] 40 University of Michigan Journal of Law Reform 569.

Reasonable Standard of Person

The reasonable standard of person is affected by two factors: a genuine lack of knowledge and conscious ignorance. As it stands today, the judiciary have taken steps through legislation and court procedures to limit the hindrance to trial proceedings. The Contempt of Court Act outlines strict repercussions where a juror unfairly influences a trial, whereas court procedures include the administration of juror oaths and affirmations to try the defendant on the evidence only.[100] In another instance, section 43 of the Criminal Justice Act 2003 enables the prosecution to apply for certain fraud cases to be conducted without a jury due to the complexity of such cases alike. Whilst both examples demonstrate how the judiciary's efforts have been somewhat effective in mitigating the effects of both a jurors' genuine lack of knowledge, and unfair influence where there has been conscious ignorance, the judiciary have been inadequate in ensuring the consistent standard of jurors. Undeniably the judiciary cannot realistically control or ensure a consistent standard of juror because each individual has different needs and capabilities, yet despite this is an area subject to strong criticism.

Such criticism has led to the suggestion of IQ testing for prospective jurors whereby that individual would have to achieve a reasonable IQ score to serve as a juror.[101] Although, this could be an inadequate solution because IQ tests are arguably a product of pseudo-psychology, which risks becoming positively discriminatory because it would refuse some members of the public on the premise of their intellect.[102] Furthermore, considering the idea of positive discrimination, it could also be said that it would be undemocratic to deny a member of public their right to perform jury service on the premise of their intellect.

---

[100]Contempt of Court Act 1981; Defence Barrister, 'Crown Court Trial Part 2 – The Jury' (*Defence Barrister*, N/D) <www.defence-barrister.co.uk/crown-court-trial-part-2-the-jury> accessed 1 September 2021.

[101]Full Fact, 'Are juries too stupid for justice?' (*Full Fact*, 22 February 2013) <www.fullfact.org/crime/are-juries-too-stupid-justice> accessed 1 September 2021.

[102]Nassim Taleb, 'Medium: IQ is a largely pseudoscientific swindle' (*Nassim Taleb.* 3 January 2019) <www.nassimtaleb.org/2019/01/iq-pseudoscientific-swindle/> accessed 1 September 2021.

On evaluation of these considerations, it is undeniably a difficult area for the judiciary and Law Commission to realistically reform.

Eliminating the Jury System

It would be reasonable to say that the practises of jury service are complicated by a multitude of contemporary issues that have arose throughout time, which could present an argument for replacing the jury system with a judge-led approach and the alternative of a hybrid approach (between a jury and judge led approach).[103]

A Judge-Led Approach

Kalven and Zeisel found that judges and juries agree on the verdict in criminal and civil cases 78% of the time, yet this still demonstrates an unacceptable discrepancy.[104] In tackling this gap, the implementation of a judge-led approach could provide a solution. A judge-led approach is common in jurisdictions such as India, Netherlands and South Africa where a judge will often hear a case and deliberate with a panel of three judges to reach a majority judgement.[105] A majority of judgements reached by their Lordships and Ladyships are central within the Supreme Court (United Kingdom), and hence raise the question as to why this cannot be the method of justice for criminal and civil trials at the Crown court too. A minority of academics have faith in a judge-only trial, but one acknowledges the advantageous position of judge-only trials in respect of the judge's legal knowledge, legal experience and

---

[103]Peter Duff, 'The limitations on trial by jury' [2001] Revue internationale de droit penal 1/2(72), 609.

[104]Harry Kalven and Hans Zeisel, 'The American Jury' [1967] Washington and Lee Law Review 24, 158-175.

[105]Ethan Lieb, 'A Comparison of Criminal Jury Decision Rules in Democratic Countries' [2007] Ohio State Journal of Criminal Law 5(629). 629 – 644.

impartiality.[106] Although, most academics are in the view that there is limited evidence to truly show the effectiveness of a judge-led justice system.[107] In addition to the limited evidence, a judge-led approach essentially violates the advantages of a jury system because a judge-led approach becomes undemocratic (to an extent), individualistic, and less equal and inclusive (given the diversity and inclusivity of the judiciary).[108] Arguably, the alternative could address the issues outlined in Section 2, but inevitably, both perspectives require a careful analysis.

A Hybrid Approach

Arguably, a judge-led approach is unfeasible, which raises the alternative of a hybrid approach. Theoretically, there are two models that the judiciary could pursue. The first model is called the collaborative model where the judge deliberates with the jury, as this would ensure "*active and meaningful*" participation in the decision-making process. Even so, this is an area of difficulty because the influence of conformity could be greater due to informational social influence (individual conforms because they believe that individual is right).[109] Conversely, the second model takes a hierarchical structure that entails the judge to deal with serious cases in comparison to the jury who deal with less-serious crimes.[110] The hier-

[106] Laura Hoyano, 'Opinion: Judge-alone trials can deliver justice – but only if defendants choose them' (*Counsel Magazine*, 5 May 2020) <www.counselmagazine.co.uk/articles/judge-alone-trials-can-deliver-justice-but-only-if-defendants-choose-them> accessed 1 September 2021.

[107] Jodie O'Leary, 'Twelve angry peers or one angry judge' [2011] Australia Criminal Law Journal 35(3), 154-169.

[108] Ministry of Justice, 'Diversity of the judiciary: 2021 statistics' (*GOV UK*, 15 July 2021) <www.gov.uk/government/statistics/diversity-of-the-judiciary-2021-statistics> accessed 2 September 2021.

[109] Morton Deutsch and Harold Gerard, 'A study of normative and informational social influences upon individual judgement' [1955] Journal of Abnormal and Social Psychology 51, 629-636.

[110] Louis Blom-Cooper, 'Judge-only trials should be an option for serious organised crimes' (The Guardian: Law, 21 May 2010) <www.theguardian.com/law/2010/may/21/judge-only-trials-option> accessed 2 September 2021.

archical model would allow the judge to deal with the complex legal issues that arise in serious cases, which ensures that a jury would be able to comprehend the evidence in less-serious cases. Nevertheless, this model does not necessarily provide a solution to unconscious conformity, UB, the logistical errors and the reasonable juror standard in any event.

In consideration of both arguments, there is seemingly no obvious way to address the multitude of factors related to the jury system. Instead, there is a clear position for retaining a 'traditional' jury in the English and Welsh jurisdiction.[111]

Conclusions

In the collation of the presented arguments, the positive critique demonstrates the jury system as standardised, collective and equal in every dimension. Although, most importantly, it is a system that is democratic and therefore becomes a legal right that belongs to a rich history engrained in the legal tradition and etiquette of England and Wales. However, the negative critique gives rise to a number of issues, including, but not limited to the influence of conformity in jury trials, unconscious bias, and the lack of geographical consistency and proportionality amongst jury representation.[112] Following, this led to the discussion of reform through a judge-led and hybrid approach.

Nonetheless, the answer to the question of whether the jury system is fit for purpose today is not simple. On evaluation of all arguments presented in this article, it appears that in its current state, the jury system is largely inadequate. All being considered, the issues of conformity and UB have a significant impact on the verdicts of jury trials. In addition, despite the factor of COVID-19, it does make one question whether the backlog of cases facing the courts is partially a product of the inefficiency of jury trials. This can largely be critiqued as a natural and inevitable consequence

[111] John Jackson, 'Unbecoming Jurors and Unreasoned Verdicts: Realising Integrity in the Jury Room' in Jill Hunter and others, *The Integrity of Criminal Process: From Theory into Practice* (Hart Publishing 2016), 307.

[112] Penrod (n69).

of the jury system, but this also complicates the position for reform further. At present, two options for the future of the jury system seem viable: (1) wilfully accepting the current issues with the system as an imperfection, or (2) reforming areas that pose issues to the current system. Ultimately, this question of whether the current jury system is fit for purpose does not have a simple solution and is seemingly more deep-rooted than anticipated, because it highlights a number of issues and gives rise to further complicated questions. Consequently, the elimination of the current jury system may seem as a far-fetched solution and suggests that reformation of the current jury system as an appropriate solution. On that note, it is important to highlight UB and conformity as good candidates for reform.

References

Adkin T., 'Guest blog: How will restricting jury trial and reducing jury numbers affect the delivery of justice?' (*The Bar Council*, 10 July 2020) <www.barcouncil.org.uk/resource/guest-blog-how-will-restricting-jury-trial-and-reducing-jury-numbers-affect-the-delivery-of-justice.html> accessed 13 August 2021.

Alschuler A., 'Racial Quotas and the Jury' (1996) DLJ 44(4).

American Psychological Association, 'APA Dictionary of Psychology: stealth juror' (*American Psychological Association*, N/D) <www.dictionary.apa.org/stealth-juror> accessed 26 August 2021.

Anwar S., Bayer P. and Hjalmarsson R., 'The Impact of Jury Race in Criminal Trials' (2012) *The Quarterly Journal of Economics* 127(2).

Aristocles (Plato), *The Republic* (≈375BC)

Aristotle, *Art of Rhetoric* (≈350 BC).

Aristotle, *Politics* (≈350 BC).

Asch S., 'Studies of independence and conformity: I. A minority of one against a unanimous majority' (1956) *Psychological Monographs: General and applied* 70(9).

Asch S., *Social Psychology* (Oxford University Press, 1952).

Bornstein B. and Greene E., 'Jury Decision Making: Implications for and From Psychology' (2011) *Sage* 20(1).

Burnkrant R. and Cousineau A., 'Informational and Normative Social Influence in Buyer Behaviour' (1975) *Journal of Consumer Research* 2(3), 207.

Daly G. and Pattenden R., 'Racial Bias and the English Criminal Trial Jury' (2005) *The Cambridge Law Journal 64*(3).

Deutsch M. and Gerard H., 'A study of normative and informational social influences upon individual judgement' (1955) *Journal of Abnormal and Social Psychology* 51.

Dicey A.V., *Introduction to the Study of the Law of the Constitution* (1885).

Duff P., 'The limitations on trial by jury' (2001) *Revue internationale de droit penal* 1/2(72).

Elek J. and Hannaford-Agor P., 'First, Do No Harm: On Addressing the Problem of Implicit Bias in Juror Decision Making' (2013) *The Journal of the American Judges Association* 404.

Ellison L. and Munro V., 'Reacting to Rape: Exploring Mock Jurors' Assessments of Complaints Credibility' (2009) *The British Journal of Criminology* 49(2).

Emmelman D., 'The Effect of Social Class on the Adjudication of Criminal Cases: Class-linked Behaviour Tendencies Common Sense and the Interpretive Procedures of Court-appointed Defence Attorneys' (1994) *Symbolic Interaction* 17(1), 1-20.

FitzGerald C. and others, 'Interventions designed to reduce implicit prejudices and implicit stereotypes in real world contexts: a systematic review' (2019) *BMC Psychology* 7(29).

Forsdyke S., 'Ancient and Modern Conceptions of the Rule of Law' (2019) University Press Scholarship Online.

Fukurai H., 'A Quota Jury: Affirmative Action in Jury Selection' (1997) *Journal of Criminal Justice* 25(6).

Gordon R. and Jacobs P., 'Forensic Psychology: Perception of Guilt and Income' (1969) *Perceptual and Motor Skills* 28(1).

Greenberg D., *Jowitts Dictionary of English Law* (5th edn., Sweet & Maxwell).

Guetzkow H., *Groups, leadership and men; research in human relations* (Carnegie Press, 1951).

Hansen M. H., *Brill's Companion to the Reception of Athenian Democracy* (Brill 2020).

Hunter J. and others, *The Integrity of Criminal Process: From Theory into Practice* (Hart Publishing 2016).

Kalven H. and Zeisel H., 'The American Jury' (1967) *Washington and Lee Law Review* 24.

Kelman H., 'Compliance, identification and internalization: three processes of attitude change' (1958) *The Journal of Conflict Resolution* 2(1).

Kemp A., 'Collaboration v Individualism: What Is Better for the Rising Academic?' (2013) *TQR* 18(50).

Kramer S.N., 'Ur-Nammu Law Code' (1954) GBP Vol. 23(1).

Lieb E., 'A Comparison of Criminal Jury Decision Rules in Democratic Countries' (2007) *Ohio State Journal of Criminal Law* 5(629).

May T. and others, 'Differential treatment in the youth justice system' (2010) Equality and Human Rights Commission Research report 50.

Miller M. and Bornstein B, 'Do juror pressures lead to unfair verdicts' (2008) *Monitor of Psychology* 39(3).

Mitchell O., 'A Meta-Analysis of Race and Sentencing Research: Explaining the Inconsistencies' (2005) JQC 21(4).

Moore S. and Newbury A., *Legal aid in crisis: Assessing the impact of reform* (Bristol University Press, 2017).

Moss P., 'Can There Be Validity without Reliability?' (1994) *AERA* 23(2).

Nadel L and Armstrong W. S., *Memory and Law* (Oxford Scholarship Online 2012).

O'Leary J., 'Twelve angry peers or one angry judge' (2011) *Australia Criminal Law Journal* 35(3).

Ormston R. and others, 'Scottish Jury Research: Findings from a Large-Scale Mock Jury Study' (2019) *Social Research Series* (10/19).

Penrod S. and Hastie R., 'A computer simulation of jury decision making' (1980) *Psychological Review* 87(2).

Reichelt J., 'Standing Alone: Conformity, Coercion, and the Protection of the Holdout Juror' (2007) 40 University of Michigan Journal of Law Reform 569.

Robertson G., 'Magna Carta and jury trial' (2015) British Library.

Ritzer G., *The Blackwell Encyclopedia of Sociology* (Blackwell Publishing 2006).

RP Advisors, *Reducing Racial Disparity in the Criminal Justice System: A Manual for Practitioners and Policymakers* (The Sentencing Project, 2008).

Salkind N.J., *Encylopedia of Research Design* (SAGE Publications 2010).

Su A., 'A Proposal to Properly Address Implicit Bias in the Jury' (2020) *Hastings Women's Law Journal 31*(1) 6.

Sunnafrank M. and Fontes N, 'General and Crime Relates Racial Stereotypes and Influence on Juridic Decisions' (1983) *Cornell Journal of Social Relations* 17(1).

Thomas C. and Balmer N., *Diversity and Fairness in the Jury System* (Ministry of Justice Research No.2, 2007).

Triandis H., *Individualism & collectivism* (1st edn, Routledge 1995).

Vidmar N. and Hans V., *American Juries: The Verdict* (Prometheus Books, 2007).

Vijer F., Hemert D. and Poortinga Y, *Multilevel Analysis of Individuals and Cultures* (Taylor & Francis 2008).

Zeigler-Hill V., Welling L. and Shackelford T., *Evolutionary Perspectives on Social Psychology* (Springer, 2015).

Waldron J., 'Is the Rule of Law an Essentially Contested Concept (in Florida)?' (2002) 21 *Law & Philosophy* 137.

Wessel E., 'Credibility of the emotional witness: a study of ratings by court judges' (2006) *Law and Human Behaviour* 30.

Parliamentary Reports

Constitution Committee, *Paper by Professor Paul Craig: The Rule of Law* (HL 2006-07).

Select Committee on the Constitution, *COVID-19 and the Courts* (HL 2019-20, 257).

Bowser A., 'To Conform or Not to Conform: An Examination of the Effects of Mock Jury Deliberation on Individual Jurors' (Electronic Theses and Dissertations, Tennessee State University 2013) 1164.

Cammack D.L., 'Rethinking Athenian Democracy' (Doctoral Dissertation, Harvard University 2013).

Gordon S., 'All Together Now: Using Principles of Group Dynamics to Train Better Jurors' (Scholarly Commons, UNLV Williams S. Boyd School of Law 2015) 896.

Koehler J., 'Train Our Jurors' (Faculty Working Papers, Northwestern University School of Law 2006) Paper 141.

Barrett and Co Solicitors, 'Will you ever be called to Jury Service?' (*Barrett & Co*, 29 August 2018) <www.barrettandco.co.uk/2018/08/29/will-you-ever-be-called-to-jury-service/> accessed 2 August 2021.

Ben Mitchell, 'Judge excused from jury service because he was presiding over case' (*The Independent,* 16 April 2020) <www.independent.co.uk/news/uk/home-news/judge-jury-service-court-trial-salisbury-winchester-keith-cutler-a8872611.html> accessed 9 December 2021

Blom-Cooper L, 'Judge-only trials should be an option for serious organised crimes' (The Guardian: Law, 21 May 2010) <www.theguardian.com/law/2010/may/21/judge-only-trials-option> accessed 2 September 2021.

D. Clark, 'Legal Aid Spending in England and Wales 2005-2020' (*Statista*, 2 November 2020) <www.statista.com/statistics/1098628/legal-aid-spending-in-england-and-wales/#statisticContainer> accessed 27 August 2021.

DaSilva D., 'The Stealth Juror' (*Jury Analyst*, 15 August 2015) <www.juryanalyst.com/blog/the-stealth-juror/> accessed 26 August 2021.

Defence Barrister, 'Crown Court Trial Part 2 – The Jury' (*Defence Barrister*, N/D) <www.defence-barrister.co.uk/crown-court-trial-part-2-the-jury> accessed 1 September 2021.

Equality and Diversity UK, 'Unconscious Bias Training Course' (*Equality and Diversity UK*, N/D) <www.equalityanddiversity.co.uk/unconscious-bias-training-course.htm> accessed 31 August 2021

Finz S., 'Peterson Prosecutors call any move to L.A. a bad trip' (*San Francisco Chronicle Archive* in *SFGATE*, May 11 2004) <www.sfgate.com/bayarea/article/REDWOOD-CITY-Peterson-prosecutors-call-any-move-2780548.php> accessed 26 August 2021.

Full Fact, 'Are juries too stupid for justice?' (*Full Fact*, 22 February 2013) <https://fullfact.org/crime/are-juries-too-stupid-justice/> accessed 1 September 2021.

GOV UK, 'Jury Service: What you can claim if you're an employee' (*GOV UK*, N/D) <https://www.gov.uk/jury-service/what-you-can-claim-if-youre-an-employee> accessed 27 August 2021.

GOV UK, 'Jury Service' (*GOV UK*, N/D) <www.gov.uk/jury-service> accessed 19 August 2021.

HM Courts & Tribunal Service, 'Guide to jury summons' (*GOV UK*, 1 July 2017) <www.gov.uk/government/publications/guide-to-jury-summons> accessed 17 August 2021.

HM Courts & Tribunals Service, "Justice Matters' (GOV UK, 8 February 2017) <www.gov.uk/government/publications/justice-matters> accessed 3 September 2021.

Hofstede Insights, 'What about the UK?' (*Hofstede Insights*, n.d.) <www.hofstede-insights.com/country/the-uk/> accessed 13 August 2021.

Hoyano L., 'Opinion: Judge-alone trials can deliver justice – but only if defendants choose them' (*Counsel Magazine*, 5 May 2020) <www.counselmagazine.co.uk/articles/judge-alone-trials-can-deliver-justice-but-only-if-defendants-choose-them> accessed 1 September 2021.

Kalven H., 'Jury' (*Britannica*, 29 March 2019) <www.britannica.-com/topic/jury> accessed 2 August 2021.

Macmillan Dictionary, 'the reasonable person' (*Macmillan dictionary*, N/D) <www.macmillandictionary.com/dictionary/british/the-reasonable-person#:~:text=UK%EE%A8%A6%20%2F%CB%8Cri%CB%90z(%C9%99),Synonyms%20and%20related%20word> accessed 26 August 2021.

Mcleod S., 'Solomon Asch – Conformity Experiment' (*Simply Psychology*, 28 December 2018) <www.simplypsychology.org/asch-conformity.html> accessed 25 August 2021

Ministry of Justice, 'Criminal court statistics quarterly, England and Wales' (*GOV UK*, 29 September 2016) <www.assets.publishing.service.gov.uk/government/uploads/system/uploads/attachment_data/file/556442/ccsq-bulletin.pdf> accessed 27 August 2021.

Ministry of Justice, 'Criminal justice statistics quarterly' (*GOV UK*, 22 August 2013) <www.gov.uk/government/collections/criminal-justice-statistics-quarterly> accessed 12 August 2021.

Ministry of Justice, 'Diversity of the judiciary: 2021 statistics' (*GOV UK*, 15 July 2021) <www.gov.uk/government/statistics/diversity-of-the-judiciary-2021-statistics> accessed 2 September 2021.

Ministry of Justice. 'Law change opens door to deaf jurors' (*GOV UK*, 9 March 2021) <www.gov.uk/government/news/law-change-opens-door-to-deaf-jurors> accessed 17 August 2021.

Rule of Law Alliance, 'Impact of Rule of Law: Rule of Law & Democracy' (*Rule of Law Alliance*, 2016) <rolalliance.org/rol-alliance-impact/rule-of-law-democracy/> accessed 10 August 2021.

Shropshire Council, Population (*Shropshire Council*, 2011) <www.shropshire.gov.uk/information-intelligence-and-insight/facts-and-figures/population> accessed 17 August 2021.

Sturge G., Court statistics for England and Wales (House of Commons Library Briefing Paper CBP 8372, 2020) <www.researchbriefings.files.parliament.uk/documents/CBP-8372/CBP-8372.pdf> accessed 22 December 2020

Taleb N., 'Medium: IQ is a largely pseudoscientific swindle' (*Nassim Taleb*. 3 January 2019) <www.nassimtaleb.org/2019/01/iq-pseudoscientific-swindle> accessed 1 September 2021.

Waldron J., 'The Rule of Law' (*Stanford Encyclopaedia of Philosophy*, 22 June 2016) <www.plato.stanford.edu/entries/rule-of-law/#Aris> accessed 9 August 2021.

Case Law

Gregory v UK (1997) 25 ECHR 577.

R v Mirza (2004) Crim 1235; (2004) 1 AC 1118.

R v Qureshi (2001) EWCA Crim 1807.

R v Smith (Lance Percival) (2003) EWCA Crim 283.

The People of the State of California v Scot Lee Peterson (2004) SC 55500.

Legislation

Contempt of Court Act 1981

Convention for the Protection of Human Rights and Fundamental Freedoms (European Convention on Human Rights, as amended).

Criminal Justice Act 2003.

Criminal Practise Directions (2015).

Juries Act 1974.

Sex Disqualification (Removal) Act 1919.

Designing Post-Genomic Future Together

Brief communication in response to the publication of the UK Government report "Genomics Beyond Healthcare"

Robert Chapman[1], Yulia Kovas[2], Fatos Selita[3]

On January 26, 2022 the UK government released a report: "Genomics Beyond Healthcare"[4]. This 198-page document considers ways in which genomic research may impact our lives outside the realm of healthcare. It provides a comprehensive overview of advances in genetics, and what they may mean for people.

It is predicted that in the next few decades during the post genomic era individuals' genetic information will be used in all spheres of life, including medicine, family, employment, education, insurance, sports, justice systems and policing. This prediction is reflected in the report, which expands the previous focus on health and medicine. The publication of the report is a great development because it examines use of genetics in a wide range of contexts and discusses both potential benefits and risks. Potential benefits and harms brought by genetic advances are also explored in a

[1]Goldsmiths, University of London.

[2]Goldsmiths, University of London; International Centre for Research in Human Development, Tomsk State University; Department of Genetics and Fundamental Medicine, Bashkir State University.

[3]Goldsmiths, University of London; International Centre for Research in Human Development, Tomsk State University. Corresponding author: Fatos Selita, Fatos.Selita@gold.ac.uk.

[4]Government Office for Science. Genomics Beyond Health. https://www.gov.uk/government/publications/genomics-beyond-health (2022).

recent book 'Oedipus Rex in the Genomic Era'[5]. The book examines, in the light of genetic knowledge, themes that date back for millennia such as free will, fate and chance; prediction, misinterpretation and the burden that comes with knowledge of the future; self-fulfilling and self-defeating prophecies; the forces that contribute to similarities and differences among people; roots and lineage; and decision making and judgement of oneself and others. It examines existential, social, ethical, and legal concerns and dilemmas introduced by the genomic era highlighting the relevance of behavioural genetics across humanities, social and life sciences. Much more work is needed to assess implications of using genetics in different contexts, including unexplored areas such as gaming and entertainment, persuasion and decision making, and gene-based life design.

The Government report is also timely as it brings into focus a growing body of research that examines people's opinions and attitudes related to the post-genomic future. The report dedicates a 4-page section to public views on genomics, concluding that "the British public can see benefits of genomic research but expresses some 'red line' concerns regarding its use" (p.170). These 'red lines' include genetic engineering, particularly to enhance human capacity; corporate or state surveillance; administrative and political usage, for example to increase controls on society; predictive insurance tests; and targeted marketing to increase profits. The report suggests that the UK public is concerned that these and other uses could disadvantage people and lead to a stratified society.

Public opinions in the UK and internationally have been a focus of our own work over the past 6 years, capturing views from people in 116 countries (see Figure 1). We have to-date analysed in depth data from 7 countries—Italy, Mexico, Nigeria, Romania, Russia, Spain, and the UK (see tagc.world). The results suggest that many people, including lawyers and judges welcome genetic applications in health care, but also some controversial applications such as for prevention of crime and gene editing to improve traits; and disagree with other applications, such as use by

[5] Kovas, Y. & Selita, F. *Oedipus Rex in the Genomic Era: Human Behaviour, Law and Society.* (Palgrave Macmillan UK, 2021).

insurance companies[6]. Views are particularly divided regarding privacy and some applications such as in sentencing[7].

Figure 1. iGLAS participant countries of residence (darker shading - more participants completed to-date.)

The opinions of wider society are essential for designing our post genomic future where all people can benefit from applications of genetic advances. Yet, to date, very few people are engaged in designing this future, and one major barrier for such engagement is poor genetic literacy. Our research showed that genetic literacy

---

[6]Selita, F., Chapman, R. & Kovas, Y. To Use or Not to Use: No Consensus on Whether and How to Apply Genetic Information in the Justice System. *Behavioral Sciences* 9, 149 (2019); Selita, F., et al. Consensus too soon: judges' and lawyers' views on genetic information use. (In Review).

[7]Selita, F., Chapman, R. & Kovas, Y. To Use or Not to Use: No Consensus on Whether and How to Apply Genetic Information in the Justice System. *Behavioral Sciences* 9, 149 (2019); Chapman, R., et al. To Tell or Not to Tell: The Ethics and Law of Disclosing Health-Related Genetic Information to Family Members. *Psych. Rus.* 11, 68–78 (2018).

is low even among the well-educated[8]. In our work as part of the Working Group on Legal, Ethical and Societal Implications of Genetics (LESIG)[9], established in 2016-17 in the UK and Russia, we also found that many lawyers in both jurisdictions did not see how new genetic advances pose risks and dilemmas, some admitting no knowledge in the area. Improving genetic literacy in societies requires engagement of the public at large, including through public dialogue, even debate, as well as changes in school and university curricula, and professional development programmes. We have seen a great shift over the past decade for psychology degrees to include genetic modules. The same needs to happen across education, law and other social sciences.

As genetic science is borderless, its impact cannot be contained within any one jurisdiction. Its regulation needs to also be borderless. The Government report recommends a unified coherent and comprehensive approach to legislating for the timely regulation of genomics in the UK. This is a necessary but challenging task for all societies, making global input particularly beneficial. For example, in our studies, contributions from the Romanian and Russian judiciaries have proven invaluable to understanding views of key stakeholders on the use of genetic information. They have also helped promote knowledge and dialogue.

Beyond legislation, in our work we have also raised that some societal structures, such as health insurance provision, will require updating, as some areas cannot be regulated by law only[10]. This means that international input is also required from other stakeholders, including sociologists, economists, policymakers and educationalists.

Our international instrument is available in several languages and is being used by research teams in many countries, including

---

[8]Chapman, R., et al. New literacy challenge for the twenty-first century: genetic knowledge is poor even among well educated. *J Community Genet* 10, 73–84 (2019); Selita, F., Smereczynska, V., Chapman, R., Toivainen, T. & Kovas, Y. Judging in the genomic era: judges' genetic knowledge, confidence and need for training. *European Journal of Human Genetics* 1–9 (2020) doi:10.1038/s41431-020-0650-8.

[9]TAGC. LESIG Working Group. tagc.world http://tagc.world/lesig/.

[10] Selita, F. Justice in the genomic and digital era: a 'different world' requiring 'different law'. *Legal issues Journal* 8, (2020).

most recently in Australia, Ecuador, and Japan. We invite researchers and practitioners in different areas from all countries to collaborate.

Jurisdictional and Technical Challenges of Next Generation Cyber Events

Peter Stephenson[1]

Abstract. On 22 December 2017 Microsoft Corporation ("MS") filed a lawsuit (Microsoft Corporation v. John Does 1-10 using IP address 73.21.204.220, (United States District Court, Western District of Washington at Seattle. Decided 2 Jan 2018, Microsoft Corp. v. Doe, CASE NO. C17-1911RSM) (the "MS case").

The suit alleges large-scale copyright infringement through software piracy and trademark infringement relative to Microsoft registered trademarks. What was unusual about this filing is that MS, at the time of filing, had nothing more on which to base its lawsuit than an IP address that had communicated over 28,000 times with its registration servers in Seattle. I discuss this in the first section discussing the MS Case.

In 2017, Kristanalea Dyroff sued Ultimate Software Group, Inc for the death of her son due to a drug overdose. She contended that her son – 29 years old at the time – was guided to a dealer of fentanyl-laced heroin based upon recommendation from Ultimate's proprietary machine learning (ML)-based tool that guided users to things on its website that might interest them. Although it could have been a major effort at applying the law to ML-based software, it failed because the judge failed to address the ML aspect directly. Instead, the court analyzed the case based upon conventional law and precedent. Likewise, the issue of personal jurisdiction in cyberspace was not, but should have been, addressed. A

[1]University of Leicester School of Law; Vidzeme University of Applied Sciences. Email: pstephen@cdfs.us

discussion with one of the attorneys for the plaintiff conducted by the author the week of 19 April 2021 confirmed that, in the attorney's opinion, the court erred in finding for the defense.

This paper analyzes the jurisdictional and technical issues raised by these two types of cyber event and postulates the jurisdictional and technical challenges raised by next generation cyber events that employ artificial intelligence ("AI"), particularly machine learning ("ML") through the lens of two cyber case analyses.

Keywords cyber, tort, jurisdiction, software piracy, copyright infringement, trademark infringement, Internet crime

Introduction to the MS Case

The filing of "John Doe" lawsuits is not uncommon. It is used frequently in cyber-related cases (See Jon BEUTLER, v. John DOE (In re <rat.com>), Circuit Court of Virginia. Nineteenth Judicial Circuit, Fairfax County) when actual defendants are, at the time of the complaint, unknown.

However, the usual purpose for filing such a lawsuit is to facilitate discovery. Should the suit continue without discovering the true identities of the Doe(s) it must be dismissed without prejudice, since service against an unknown party cannot be made. Further, no injunction can be made against an unknown party.

Since discovery must be made relative to a case pending – i.e., a complaint and summons issued to the defendant (See "Federal Rules of Civil Procedure (USA), Title II, Rule 4. Summons) – the John Doe suit is useful only for obtaining defendant identity.

The current case states in relevant part (Section II paragraph 3 at line 25):

The true identities of Defendants are not presently known to Microsoft. On information and belief, Defendants are in possession or control of the Internet Protocol ("IP") address 73.21.204.220 ("the subject IP Address") and have used it to further the unlawful conduct alleged herein.

This poses intertwined technical and jurisdictional challenges. This section will explore those challenges.

Jurisdiction and Venue

MS claims personal jurisdiction over the Does based upon several theories. The complaint says, in relevant part,

Civil actions, suits, or proceedings arising under any Act of Congress relating to copyrights or exclusive rights in mask works or designs may be instituted in the district in which the defendant or his agent resides or may be found (See 28 U.S.C. § 1400(a)).

MS also claims personal jurisdiction based upon Brayton Purcell LLP v. Recordon & Recordon (See Brayton Purcell LLP v. Recordon & Recordon, 606 F.3d 1124 (9th Cir. 2010)):

This circuit interprets this provision to allow venue in any judicial district where, if treated as a separate state, the defendant would be subject to personal jurisdiction.

Finally, MS states, again, in relevant part,

Venue is also proper in this district pursuant to 28 U.S.C. 1391(b) because a substantial part of the events giving rise to the claims occurred in the Western District of Washington.

28 U.S.C. 1391(b) reads:

> **(b) Venue in general.** -- A civil action may be brought in—
>
> **(1)** a judicial district in which any defendant resides, if all defendants are residents of the State in which the district is located;
>
> **(2)** a judicial district in which a substantial part of the events or omissions giving rise to the claim occurred, or a substantial part of property that is the subject of the action is situated; or
>
> **(3)** if there is no district in which an action may otherwise be brought as provided in this section, any judicial district in which any defendant is subject to the court's personal jurisdiction with respect to such action.

On the surface it would appear that MS has a valid point regarding personal jurisdiction. However, a careful reading of the citations in the complaint tells a somewhat different story. The reasons are technical, based upon the basics of cyber science, and demonstrate an instance where knowledge of these basics would be helpful.

Cyber science is defined as:

> Cyber science is the study of phenomena caused or generated within the cyber space, which may or may not interact with phenomena caused or generated within the physical space (Peter R. Stephenson, Defining a Cyber Jurisprudence (2017). Definition 1).

In MS we see a combination of phenomena caused or generated within the cyber space and phenomena caused or generated within the physical space. It is clear that the physical space phenomina comprise the theft of intellectual property belonging to MS and the unauthorized registration of that intellectual property on an MS server located in Seattle.

What is not clear is where the Does reside. There is no guarantee that, simply because the IP address alleged by MS is, in fact, being used by Does who reside in the United States, complicating the jurisdictional issues as presented by MS. In fact, it is quite conceivable that the Does reside in some other part of the world and have hijacked the server at the IP address in the complaint. This is an action generated within the cyberspace. It demands a more thorough analysis of the address itself.

Because the complaint is filed largely with the intent of facilitating discovery, we may assume that (1) MS was not able to find out who the Does are through the owner of the address (Comcast) or, (2), that Comcast does not know who the Does are and deeper investigation is required. It is most likely that Comcast has not provided user information to MS and will not do so without a subpoena to prevent violations of its customers' privacy based upon a fishing expedition by MS (See State v. Reid, 194 N.J. 386, 945 A.2d 26 (2008) – this is one of the most-often cited cases on the topic of ISP subscriber policy. It requires, based upon the New Jersey Constitution, a subpoena prior to the surrender of subscriber information by the ISP.).

That the court has subject matter jurisdiction is clear from the citations by MS in the complaint (See 15 U.S.C. § 1121, 17 U.S.C. § 501, and 28 U.S.C. §§ 1331 and 1338(a)).

Technical Considerations

The technical considerations in MS are part and parcel of the jurisdictional issues because there is no guarantee that the Does are residents of any forum in which the court would have personal jurisdiction. Some of the considerations are:

- Are the Does direct users (subscribers) of the IP address?
- Have the Does hijacked the IP address which, in fact, is assigned to a legitimate user?
- Is the IP address static or dynamic? If dynamic, was it the only address allegedly used for the alleged infringements?
- Is the IP address in use by a home user or a business? Who has access to the computer(s) connected to the address?
- Is the IP address the Internet-facing element of a back-end computer network?
- If the IP address is connected to a back-end computer network, of what does the network consist? Are firewalls and other security measures in place?
- Is the IP address the actual IP address or has it been "spoofed"?

Recognizing that the complaint is for facilitating discovery and issuing a subpoena to which Comcast will need to respond, a detailed analysis of the computer(s) related to the IP address is necessary. The complaint reads in relevant part:

The true identities of Defendants are not presently known to Microsoft. On information and belief, Defendants are in possession or control of the Internet Protocol ("IP") address 73.21.204.220 ("the subject IP Address") and have used it to further the unlawful conduct alleged herein.

Further, it may not be reasonable for the technical reasons to assert personal jurisdiction over all ten Does. There is no evidence that all ten Does participated in the same events that triggered the complaint and thus the joinder of the defendants would be improper (See Hard Drive Prods., Inc. v. Does 1-188, 809 F. Supp. 2d 1150 (N.D. Cal. 2011)).

The presence of the technical considerations suggested by the MS complaint tend to make the complaint too broad.

A plaintiff may sue a defendant using a fictitious name when she knows the defendant's general identity but cannot, without further discovery, determine the defendant's true name. In this situation: ... The plaintiff must provide a description that is sufficient to permit the defendant to be served with process (Complaint (Federal) RESOURCE ID 9-507-9951, Thompson, Reuters (2017)).

This specificity in the naming of John Doe defendants is well-settled. See, for example, Keno v. Doe which reads in relevant part (Keno v. Doe, 74 F.R.D. 587 (D.N.J. 1977), aff'd, 578 F.2d 1374 (3d Cir. 1978)),

This ruling in no way involves the long-known and well-established practice of naming parties by fictitious names, such as "John Doe", when the real name of the party is not known. See, for example, Bivens v. Six Unknown Agents, 403 U.S. 388, 91 S.Ct. 1999, 29 L.Ed.2d 619 (1971). In such cases, however, the complaint should state that the name is fictitious and provide an adequate description of some kind which is sufficient to identify the person involved so that process can be served.

Given the vague description of the Doe defendants in the complaint (*...On information and belief, Defendants are in possession or control of the Internet Protocol ("IP") address 73.21.204.220*), make it difficult or impossible to identify the ten Doe defendants with certainty.

Finally, it is not possible, from the information provided in the complaint, to determine whether the Does were operators of remote computers simply offering a gateway to mailicious (or other) users or did they participate directly in the thefts.

Conclusions Relative to the MS Case

While we do not argue with the need to address software piracy and copyright/trademark infringement, especially where the Internet is involved, we think that this complaint is likely not to lead to a successful conclusion beyond the court allowing MS to take control of the applicable servers. We find the identification of the Doe defendants too broad and vague to be useful, especially when the defendants must be named more explicitly.

The technical considerations implicit and explicit in the facts of the case as presented by MS in the complaint are complicated and ambiguous. While we accept that the purpose of the complaint may be to permit discovery that can lead to the identification of the defendants, its overbroad nature will make the resulting investigation little more than a fishing expedition. It gives the appearance that the goal is the takedown of the impacting servers.

We suspect that, given the resources available to MS, there could be considerable more data available. For example, the complaint refers to MS use of cyberforensics (Complaint at E 29):

In order to combat the global threat of software piracy of its software, Microsoft relies on state-of-the-art technology to detect software piracy called "cyberforensics."

The complaint goes on (Complaint at E 30):

Through cyberforensics, Microsoft analyzes activation data voluntarily provided by users when they activate Microsoft software, including the IP address from which a given product is activated. An IP address is a numerical identifier used to uniquely identify an internet-capable device when the device is connected to the Internet. An IP address is ordinarily assigned to an internet user (whether an individual or an entity) by the user's Internet Service Provider ("ISP").

This is misleading because, under certain circumstances, IP addresses are assigned automatically based upon connection to the ISP server and are rotated periodically. While it is true that logs are kept of these rotations, IP address use is by no means consistent, especially if an unauthorized user takes pains to obfuscate his or her actual use. Further, it is relatively simple to "spoof" any IP address, making it look as if the source is somewhere it is not.

Given the level of cyberforensics and the breadth of MS's reach across the global Internet, it should not be difficult to provide more information, perhaps making it more difficult for the Doe defendants ultimately to prevail.

Next Generation Cyber Events Generally

In his paper on adversarial machine learning and the law (Peter Stephenson, Adversarial Machine Learning: The Coming Legal Storm, 8 Legal Issues Journal (2020)), Stephenson posits a hypothetical cyber attack where next generation machine learning bots constitute the cause in fact. However, the proximate cause must be the hacker who programmed the bots. Testing for proximate cause we may use the "but-for" test or the "substantial factor" test.

For example, but for the programmer's code the bots would not have attacked the bank (Stephenson's hypothetical describes a next generation attack on a bank that resulted in exfiltration of millions of dollars). Likewise, the programmer's code was the substantial factor in the attack on the bank. Thus, we may establish both cause in fact and proximate cause.

To understand how this attack is both similar to and distinct from the MS case, we must look at some cyber definitions.

The MS case involved theft of intellectual property initiated by ten bots or direct attacks from command and control ("C2") servers. The human selects the target and loads the script to direct the attack.

These C2 servers generally are part of a bullet-proof hosting network. This type of network uses obfuscation measures that make it extremely difficult to trace the actual C2 servers. The key point to understand, however, is that C2 servers of this type are controlled directly by a human attacker. They are automated extensions of the intruder's hacking skills.

Next generation attacks – or, as we will refer to them hereafter, "events" to cover those malicious activities that cannot be classed as "attacks" as well as actual attacks – do not involve human control once the code has been written and launched.

Some Terms

In this case there are four next generation concepts with which one should be familiar: hivenets, swarmbots, machine learning (ML) and blockchain.

A hivenet may be thought of as a "collective" much as the Star Trek enemy, the Borg. It is a central controlling intelligence created by the programmer to direct an army of swarmbots in performing their mission.

Manky gives us the following definition of hivenets and swarmbots (Derek Manky, The Evolving Threat Landscape - Swarmbots, Hivenets, Automation in Malware, CSO Online(2018)):

The benefit of a hivenet is that the swarmbots can reason collectively using data collected by the individuals. The hive learns through machine learning and once trained initially – perhaps using semi-supervised training to get a head start defining the parameters of the bot master's intended mission. The swarm then can seek victims and gather its assigned data communicating with each other and, ultimately, the bot master – now the hive master - without using a C2

In our scenario, the hivenet is a machine learning program that is programmed specifically with the mission of exfiltrating money from the victim's bank account. Swarmbots communicate with the hive to update the data set and receive new instructions. All of this is done without human intervention.

ML is a form of artificial intelligence where the program, using one or more defining algorithms, learns to make decisions similar to the way a human would. Specifically, it is defined by *Expert System* as

Machine learning is an application of artificial intelligence (AI) that provides systems the ability to automatically learn and improve from experience without being explicitly programed (Expert System, What is machine learning? A definition, Expert System(2017), available at https://expertsystem.com/machine-learning-definition).

We can further define a machine learning algorithm mathematically as (Master Machine Learning Algoritims - Discover How They Work and How to Implement Them from Scratch (Jason Brownlee. 2019))

$$Y = f(X)$$

Which simply means that the result of a machine learning algorithm (Y) is some function or formula (f) times the given independent variable (X). These ML algorithms do not yield absolute (deterministic) results. Rather, the results are the likelihood of the result being correct (probabalistic). The function f can be quite complicated and there can be multiple fs. So, while the theory is simple, the practice is complicated.

Applying the formula to an ML-based attack, one can see the process easily. Recalling that *Y* is a dependent variable (the solution we seek) and *X* is the independent variable (the data we have) we turn to *f*, the modifying function. There may be several *f*s, but once they are established, they form the basis for completing the equation.

In an ML-powered attack, the independent variables are used to train and refine *f*. There are many independent variables and we derive new dependent variables for use each time it encounters a new *X*. Once the training is complete, we refer to the result as a model. The model encounters data (*X*), applies *f*, and calculates a new *Y*.

The swarmbots approach a target, analyze it, apply knowledge from the hive, or "collective", and develop a solution. The solution is reported back to the hive and it becomes useful to the rest of the swarm. All of this is done without human intervention once the model is trained.

The blockchain is a nearly irreversable communication and data management method of peer-to-peer of journaling and communication. It is the encrypted communication and management method used for trading cryptocurrency such as bitcoin. However, it has many other uses such as obscuring IP addresses.

The problem of jurisdiction

Stephenson discusses the issue of jurisdiction in cyberspace in his PhD dissertation (unpublished - Peter Stephenson, A Framework for Determining U.S. Jurisdiction in Cyberspace (2019) University of Leicester, School of Law) as well as in his published paper on adversarial machine learning. The problem is focused on identifying the responsible entity in an AI or ML-powered event. Is the responsible entity the programmer who created the hive and the swarm? Is it the hivemaster who gave the hive its mission?

And once identified, where is the proper jurisdiction? It could be the launch point for the event. This could be in an entirely different jurisdiction from that of the hivemaster. For example, if the hive/attack is launched by a hacker in Ukrane using code that is resident on Amazon Web Services ("AWS") which is the logical candidate for jurisdiction? This challenge exists today with current generation attacks, such as the MS attack described above. The difference is that the C2 servers are the sources of the attack and those servers have administrators, no matter how well hidden. In an AI or ML-driven attack no such convenience exists becase no C2 servers exist.

To address this challenge, Stephenson suggests a three-prong analysis for determining jurisdiction in cyberspace:

1. *The Cyber Event Test, and...*
2. *The Modifier Test, and...*
3. *The Cyber Effects Test*

In order to be classified as a Cyber Event, the case must adhere to both the definition of cyberspace (Cyberspace is a complex global information infrastructure that facilitates communication between technology such as computers, networks and other digital systems, both independently and on behalf of people using it. Cyberspace per se is distinct from physical space and the constraints imposed by it such as geographic boundaries (Stephenson)) *and the definition of cyber science* (Cyber science is the study of phenomena caused or generated within the cyber space, which may or may not interact with phenomena caused or generated within the physical space (Stephenson)) *(the Cyber Event Test).*

In order to be subject to jurisdiction in cyberspace, the case must demonstrate purposeful availment within the context of cyberspace (the Modifier Test).

In order to be subject to jurisdiction in cyberspace the case must be able to apply the standard effects test within the context of cyberspace (the Cyber Effects Test).

This is not a cure-all for the jurisdicitonal challenge – how does one prove purposful availment, when the hivemaster may not have provable knowledge of the target(s) of the attack?

Introduction to the Dyroff Case

Kristanalea Dyroff sued the Ultimate Software Group Inc. (Dyroff v. Ultimate Software Grp., Inc., No. 17-CV-05359-LB, 2017 WL 5665670 (N.D. Cal. Nov. 26, 2017), aff'd, 934 F.3d 1093 (9th Cir. 2019)) for (1) negligence, (2) wrongful death, (3) premises liability, (4) failure to warn, (5) civil conspiracy, (6) unjust enrichment and (7) violation of the Drug Dealer Liability Act in the death of her son,

29-year old Wesley Greer from an overdose of heroin laced with fentanyl. Ultimate Software moved, successfully, to dismiss all charges.

Today, there are almost no cases where ML or AI participate in the direct cause. Although, it is becoming increasingly common to see them show up in proximate cause. Such is the case here.

Plaintiff claims that her son would not have been directed to a drug dealer and a deadly dose of illicit drugs if a propriety algorithms did not suggestions based data mined from user posts. Those data presumably formed the training dataset for the model. Since such models are created by people, bias enters the picture ("Bias in Machine Learning is defined as the phenomena of observing results that are systematically prejudiced due to faulty assumptions." Jaspreet, Understanding and Reducing Bias in Machine Learning, Towards Data Science(2019)). This is a clear case of bias in the ML model. However, the court did not acknowledge this and granted the dismissal holding that:

1 operator was entitled to immunity under Communications Decency Act (CDA);

2 website's anonymity feature and website operator's public statements were insufficient to plausibly allege collusion with drug dealers; and

3 operator had no duty to warn users.

Plaintiff's first count - negligence - likely could have addressed the bias in the ML model. In 2019, the data science community understood the concept of bias in the model, however, the court seemed not to. Negligence stems from an ordinary duty of care under California law. In this case, the use of an ML model to steer users to particular vendors or discussion groups could be construed as generating a duty of care to base recommendations on an unbiased model.

However, the court held that, "...Ultimate Software's use of the *neutral tools and functionalities* on its website did not create a risk of harm that imposes an ordinary duty of care. (emphasis added)" The difficulty with that holding is that the tools and functionalities were not neutral. In fact they contained inherent bias that should have changed the court's viewpoint to a duty of care out of which could rise a finding of negligence.

Jurisdiction is another point of confusion in cyber cases such as this one. The Three Prong Analysis might shed some jurisdictional light here, although peer-reviewed, this analysis certainly is subject to debate.

The case was brought in the United States District Court, N.D. California, San Francisco Division. Presumably, although the case does not state specifically, both plaintif and defendant appear to reside within the court's jurisdiction. However, the fact is that Ultimate Software Group's ("USG") headquarters is in Florida. From this, a jurisdiction issue arises, since the "Experience Project" – USG's website – was cloud-based, therefore, it is not easy to locate it physically.

We begin with the first prong in answering the question as to whether the California court had personal jurisdiction.

The Cyber Event Test

The Cyber Event Test states,

> In order to be classified as a Cyber Event, the case must adhere to both the definition of cyberspace and the definition of cyber science.

This clearly is a cyber event since it exists whollly in cyberspace and is a phenomenon caused or generated within cyberspace (the web site).

This meets the test.

The Modifier Test

The Modifier Test states,

> In order to be subject to jurisdiction in cyberspace, the case must demonstrate purposeful availment within the context of cyberspace.

The web site owner purposely availed itself of access to users who met certain profiles generated by its ML tools. This suggests that the proper jurisdiction may be Florida and that the California court may not have had jurisdiction. Further, the web site was an active – as opposed to a passive or "brochure" – site. In fact, there were multiple specific contacts between Florida (or the web site owned by the Florida corporation) and the plaintiff to establish purposeful availment. There can be an argument that Florida – not California – was the proper jurisdiction.

The Cyber Effects Test

The Cyber Effects Test states,

> In order to be subject to jurisdiction in cyberspace, the case must be able to apply the standard effects test within the context of cyberspace.

It is not disputed that the plaintiff was the party affected by the web site.

This meets the test.

While it is arguable that the California court might be challenged on jurisdiction, often the effects test is the determinant in such cases. It appears that the California court may or may not have been correct.

Conclusion

Today, there are very few cases that involve AI or ML-enabled cyber events. Virtually all are copyright infringement, patent infringement and cases such as the above. That is not a permanent state of affairs, however. As more and more actors become proficient in next generation techniques, current generation cyber events are expected to evolve.

Trend Micro, in a recent report (Malicious Uses and Abuses of Artificial Intelligence. (2020)) listed at least eight specific areas sensitive to next generation abuse:

– AI-supported authentication compromise

– AI-aided encryption

– Human impersonation (deepfake)

– AI-supported hacking

– Content generation

– Remote ML learning sets polution

– AI-enabled stock market manipulation

– AI-supported ransomware

The report lists several more as well.

Today's laws, investigatory techniques and trained cyber-legal professionals are not ready for the coming wave of adversarial uses of artificial intelligence. Indeed, developers of protective systems that can detect and interdict malicious AI and ML-enabled events struggle to stay ahead of the current generation attacks.

For example, even the use of sophisticated ML-based cyber security tools has been shown to be susceptable to various forms of adversarial machine learning. Likewise, determining personal jurisdiction in these cases is not straightforward.

Bibliography

Microsoft Corporation v. John Does 1-10 using IP address 73.21.204.220, (United States District Court, Western Disctrict of Washington at Seattle).

Jon BEUTLER, v. John DOE (In re <rat.com>), (Circuit Court of Virginia. Nineteenth Judicial Circuit, Fairfax County).

"Federal Rules of Civil Procedure (USA), Title II, Rule 4. Summons

28 U.S.C. § 1400(a)

Brayton Purcell LLP v. Recordon & Recordon, 606 F.3d 1124 (9th Cir. 2010)

Peter R. Stephenson, Defining a Cyber Jurisprudence (2017).

State v. Reid, 194 N.J. 386, 945 A.2d 26 (2008)

15 U.S.C. § 1121, 17 U.S.C. § 501, and 28 U.S.C. §§ 1331 and 1338(a)

Hard Drive Prods., Inc. v. Does 1-188, 809 F. Supp. 2d 1150 (N.D. Cal. 2011)

MS Complaint (Federal) RESOURCE ID 9-507-9951, THompson, Reuters(2017), available at https://intl-westlaw-com.ezproxy3.lib.le.ac.uk/Document/I0f9fc042e-f0811e28578f7ccc38dcbee/View/FullText.html?originationContext=document&transitionType=DocumentItem&contextData=(sc.Search)#co_anchor_a514141.

Keno v. Doe, 74 F.R.D. 587 (D.N.J. 1977), aff'd, 578 F.2d 1374 (3d Cir. 1978)

Peter Stephenson, Adversarial Machine Learning: The Coming Legal Storm, 8 LEGAL ISSUES JOURNAL (2020).

Derek Manky, The Evolving Threat Landscape - Swarmbots, Hivenets, Automation in Malware, CSO Online(2018), available at https://www.csoonline.com/article/3301148/the-evolving-threat-landscape-swarmbots-hivenets-automation-in-malware.html.

Expert System, What is machine learning? A definition, Expert System (2017), available at https://expertsystem.com/machine-learning-definition/.

Jason Brownlee, Master Machine Learning Algorithms - Discover How They Work and How to Implement Them from Scratch (Jason Brownlee. 2019).

Peter Stephenson, A Framework for Determining U.S. Jurisdiction in Cyberspace (2019) University of Leicester, School of Law.

Dyroff v. Ultimate Software Grp., Inc., No. 17-CV-05359-LB, 2017 WL 5665670 (N.D. Cal. Nov. 26, 2017), aff'd, 934 F.3d 1093 (9th Cir. 2019)

Jaspreet, Understanding and Reducing Bias in Machine Learning, Towards Data Science(2019), available at https://towardsdatascience.com/understanding-and-reducing-bias-in-machine-learning-6565e23900ac.

Malicious Uses and Abuses of Artificial Intelligence. (2020).

Legal Issues Journal

www.legalissuesjournal.com
editor@uklsa.co.uk

The United Kingdom Law and Society Association

To support the Journal or UKLSA in general,
email president@uklsa.co.uk.

www.uklsa.co.uk

www.ingramcontent.com/pod-product-compliance
Lightning Source LLC
LaVergne TN
LVHW022108200926
848481LV00003B/1104

* 9 7 9 8 2 1 5 0 3 3 4 1 8 *